An Epic of Job

THE BIBLICAL WARRIOR-PRIEST

WRITTEN BY:

DAVID BEN FOSTER

Copyright© 2016 David Ben Foster

ISBN: 978-0-9864010-7-7
Library of Congress Control Number: 2016905219

All rights reserved. Except for use in any review, the reproduction or utilization of this work in whole or in part in any form by any electronic, mechanical or other means, now known or hereafter invented, including xerography, photocopying and recording, or in any information storage or retrieval system, is forbidden without the written permission of the author.

**Blossom
Book Publishing**
A Division of Blossom Marketing & Publishing, LLC

Published by Blossom Book Publishing
Medina, Ohio

Printed in the United States of America

DEDICATION

I dedicate this book to the people who encouraged me to stay the course and continue writing. The loves of my life, my wife Catherine, and our daughter Emma and son, David Ben II.

Without their encouragement and steadfast urging, I could not have remained diligent to this twenty year endeavor.

PROLOGUE

An Epic of Job, The Biblical Warrior-Priest is fictionally, symbolically, and allegorically based on the Book of Job in the Old Testament. This work has taken about fifteen years. The first thirty-three pages were written in 2001. Research on Philo of Alexandria, early Christians like Origin and Saint Ambrose, and scholars in the fields of symbolism, imagery, allegory, and parables had been an extensive study.

I have been writing poetry for more than fifty years, so what first interested me about Job, had been the poetry, but more specifically the poetry found in the speeches of Job, Eliphaz, Bildad, Zophar, and God.

I had been surprised to discover that Uz, near Damascus was about twenty-four thousand acres, based on the count of the sheep, camels, oxen, and donkeys. Job had probably traded as far away as India and Egypt on the Damascus trade routes. Job had certainly been a wealthy man.

One book in the Old Testament, *The Song of Solomon*, written by Solomon, is sexually suggestive, and according to some scholars, is an allegory of God's love for Israel. Philo, a Jewish philosopher from Alexandria, a contemporary of Christ, believed that interpreting the Old Testament through the lens of non-literal allegory is a good way to discover truth. He also used symbolism when interpreting or analyzing the Septuagint. This Greek text of the Old Testament had been use extensively by Hellenized Jews.

Job is a good Old Testament book to allegorize. As an allegorical work, *An Epic of Job*, is primarily fictionalized, but contains elements of truth. Job had been a real man; wealthy above most men in the Damascus area based on the multitude of animals and land mass. He had been caught in the middle of a debate between God and Satan; suffered unjustly; all ten of his children had been killed; he had been restored to complete health; God doubled his wealth; and he had ten more children. There are two great truths in Job: "If a man dies, shall he live again? All the days of my appointed time, I will wait, till my change comes. You shall call, and I will answer...For I know that my redeemer lives, and he shall stand at the latter day upon the earth; and though after my skin, worms destroy this body, yet in my flesh shall I see God" (Job 14:14,15; 19:25,26). The second is like the conclusion in Solomon's work: "Behold, the fear of the Lord, that is wisdom, and to depart from evil, is understanding" (Job 28:28).

Satan, the Devil, former Lucifer, and Dark, as I had named him, is first found in Genesis, speaking to a naïve Eve. King David asks God to send Satan to his enemies, and countless other times, Dark is directly involved with man and God. In the one chapter in the New Testament book of Jude, Dark is mentioned arguing with the Archangel Michael.

The patriarchal period was pre-Moses and his laws. Job is a patriarch, and heads of families during this period served as priests, such as the patriarchal warrior King of Salem and priest, Milchizedec who had helped Abraham defeat several other kings, and then blessed him with wine and bread. Afterward, Abraham gave him a tenth of his bounty. This is recorded in the book of Genesis.

Job, as most Israelite young men in all probability, had been required to battle enemies. I recreated him as a super hero—different than Gideon or Samson. Following his military service, he had become the patriarchal head of his large family, and he served as priest. In the beginning of the book, Job offers sacrifices to God in behalf of his family as had other patriarchal heads of families.

These are the reasons I had made *An Epic of Job* an allegorical, fictional, and analogical work: making Job the warrior-priest.

David Ben Foster

An Epic of Job, The Biblical Warrior-Priest

INVOCATION

This supplication lifted to my Light
is framed to praise and honor righteous might
in all of life—loss and gain, woe and joy.
I, in awe, covered with dust, must employ
this private prayer, and bow my lowly heart
as priest before Your holy thrown; impart
to me a blameless state, although my soul
deserves much pain, as love staves off Sheol.
An archangel, three times has spoken out
against my thoughts with clatter and shout
to shatter my mind as I'd blackout.
but as quickly, my muse steals into silence doubt
to watch my unjust suffering—the source
of sin and misery against me; remorse
as soldier, a spoiler of life and land
defeating large armies, a firebrand
of killing, but bravely killing, daring
men who had been twice my size, then tearing
these enemies of Light into pieces
of bloody parts that ever increases
my valor and honor; recognition of
my leadership carried everywhere of
exploits, exceptional ability,
that others could not fathom, nor equal;
yet, fighting men on foot with visceral
skill, many sought me out; came to join me
for all challenges especially to be
in battle against Dark, for nothing could

deter my passion. An Archangel stood
beside me named Michael—I could not lose.
I had refused to neutralize or to defuse,
for I was not there to sue for peace,
but rather for victory's sweet release

Affirm this frail attempt to plead my cause,
as reflection of Your immutable laws
and steadfast love, for I, the living mud
whose impermanent blue veins route a flood
to my brain, with willingness to proceed,
but save me, if Your servant's ink should bleed
with favor; then could this high task succeed.
I knew well the Divine-given talent to
be triumphant over Dark, nor ensue—
could his minions, against the measure of
Your impregnable power. You, above
all gods grant spirit to able-bodied
men who you had awesomely embodied
with the art of war: experts with shield, sword,
and spear; although I had been, by your word,
the chief of all men of war—none like me.
At last, You had chosen me, your priest—me,
who by your request, I laid down weapons
to farm a modest farm, but it siphons
my spirit dry, yet I care for my large
family, drink wine with friends, and charge
each day across this land remembering
times past, each child born, like a revolving
in my head that makes the clouds spin about
until I sit alone in the field; doubt
creeps in like a viper beneath my bed—

it causes me to ponder about war:
a man said today, warning the kingdom
like a prophet—his prophesies seldom,
correct—that war was indeed approaching
and we, all or in part, with resounding
fury, would perish as horsemen with swords
would strike us down as though sheep. The lords
in the land tended to disagree and
went home, yet fear swept through the narrow land,
and I, covered in dread like a man facing
death. Hot breath stuck to my tongue—heart racing;
I returned home to gaiety, drinking,
and games; but no time for priestly scolding.

Foreboding uncertainty blankets
me tonight—Light, tell me of my benefits
for I see little hope, and I am out
of fight; give rest to my sorrowful doubt,
or invigorate me to accomplish more
than before—I call for a greater chore.
I am not like the fallen souls in days
past, like Nephilim humans, for their ways
I do not like; raise me up to greater
exploits; to strike down beasts with saber
on land and sea. Dark is a seductive
salesman, wicked, utterly corruptive.
This satanic spirit wishes me dead;
he bargained with You for my soul; he said
that his goal was Lucifer's redemption;
it is I who must win a prevention
to save myself from death, and to prove my
service to You, Righteous Lord. So then why

must this bargain in the heavens mold me?
Double my strength and verve; let liars be.
You are a God of pure omnipotence;
and a most holy God with omniscience.
Empower me with virtuous valor;
let every evil spirit, potent man conjure
alarm and quickly take flight before me;
for if this prophet is correct, agree
with me and bless this man of yours who prays
covered with sackcloth and ashes; displays
an utter dependence on You, my Rock.
I rest with confidence: and when the cock
crows at morning light, permit me to rise
in a form greater than my youth; my eyes
will marvel at this view; transformed so
valiant. I'm grateful in the hollow
of your hand, for hope expects more because
of who You are; I'll defend for Your cause
as I'm reinforced with divine power
I can but succeed; You're my watchtower.

An Epic of Job, The Warrior-Priest

CANTO ONE

Stanza 1

*I*n Uz there dwelled a blameless man; his soul
abhorred what seemed appearances of sin,
whether it be a thing or from within;
he was a farmer, and a priest,
Cosmos crowned him greatest in the near east.
His quiver full with Heaven's sacred whole;
seven sons who shared his wealth—not creed,
burning their nights for days; ungrateful seed;
they denied, "…not idle times, but a feast."
with means in a kingdom that only increased.
Their vision had no length in life—no goal.
Unlike the three daughters who had union
with firm resolve, foreign to confusion,
beauty was their vice; Crypris envied these
goddesses, but dare not ever displease,
for vengeance was warning enough; she flit
temptations like a gorgeous nymph, away
without words, reserving spleen, in a ray
of golden light, leaving pastoral scene
and lovely virgins unblemished, serene.
Preparing daily for a feast, they'd sit
in bathes of imported oils; mirth lifted
beyond the walls, as birds sang their gifted
response. Applying kohl to darken dark,
radiant eyes; rare cosmetics—no mark
or blemish to cover; but useless it

was to remind them: Nature indeed their
benefactor had reassured such care.
They knew quite well that vanity adorned
such occasions—still hair line wrinkles—mourned.
Word of their loveliness ferried
beyond local suitors who but harried
them, but such paramours never tarried.

Stanza 2

The feasts began beneath a waiting sun;
their hair was fine, soft, ebony, pulled back
as devoted sun kissed their crowns of black
in flashes as they strolled the meadow near
the stream lined with trees; they could see and hear
in the air the birds—loved by everyone
in those quiet thousand hills of Uz.
"Siblings sound alike in gaiety," was
smiled by a guest, that brought smiles, anything
caused them to laugh, giggle, feel high, or sing—
for boredom had a few faces, but fun
consumed them, but it worried Father-
priest who had built altars for each, a bother
made necessary as sin had progressed.
Early mornings were heavy on his breast;
faith sacrificed for sin unknown, or known
brought peace of mind, assurance for his own
offspring—wayward, happy, bones of his bone.
The Patriarch in countryside, shared love,
tranquility, quiet busyness of
an attentive servant; yet alone

in his paradise south of the Dead Sea
in a garden wide, with much to oversee.
Obedient, an upright man, holy
in God's gaze, sought to please, but was lowly.
His kingdom was unmovable, lone
determination, like a soldier, Light
knew well Job's meekness, devotion, foresight;
Job rejoiced in dance and vowed to sever
unrighteousness, life's greatest endeavor.
His land had seven thousand sheep to call;
four thousand more submissive beasts, in all;
seasons changed nothing, just good would befall.

CANTO TWO

Stanza 3

Entering the perfect Light were Light's sons,
battle healed, strong, who marched in duty
on appointed days, bringing their booty—
exploits of goodness and feats of honor,
unlike the defeated who tasted dishonor.
Emasculated, forsaken, Light shuns
them still to celestial's surprise,
except to Judge's with omniscient eyes.
Adversary enters this divine scene;
his twisted sneer undeniably seen
as he strode to the thrown among ones
who readied in a circle for an insult
that might at once be spit out. They heard, "Halt.
Parade-rest." Satan, not general then,
eternally scarred warriors had been
maddened, separated; fixed fault for ones
commanded to remain below; engaged
to taunt or tempt the fallen enraged.
As was proper, Light spoke first to the guest
knowing His latitude, questioned his guest;
victors listened for insults; beaten ones
listened; Dark grimly stated travels,
"Back and forth on earth I move…" unravels
his misery, but checks his bitter tongue
suddenly with cautious intent, strung
out in poetic form; shocked holy ones.

Then Light interrupts His Adversary
checking his point, though unnecessary,
by asking if he knew of Job, His righteous,
upright, servant, truly conscientious,
who lived in Uz as priest, where life was ease
in gardens of peace as riches increase;
for he prays often to me—Giver of lease.

Stanza 4

"Of course, why would he fear You? His lush dream
property is hemmed in with holy cloth
freely given, and does not lend to sloth?
A virtue omitted? An oversight?
Man, since Eden's great gates clanged closed, was quite
cursed to till in sweat, ever stained. You deem
Job, this upright shepherd, an exception
to Adam's bent soul? Condemnation
passes over him, or am I missing
something crucial to humble surmising?"
But Light said nothing, knowing Dark's scheme.
"Toil is hardly what his hands do, for mere
touch increased blessings; no severe
loss tested his fear You, nor wavered
his faith; but, strip him of all he's savored,
those idle years beneath selective dream,
and he will awaken to deny You
as precious wealth evaporates as dew."
Then Light acknowledged the challenge in calm,
calculated certainty; lifted His palm

in acceptance of the Tempter's ill scheme
to decree: "Put your hand to all his worth,
but spare his life; destroy his spirit's mirth,
and by such fierce fire, see a priest's rebirth;
no other warnings—now return to earth."
Satan was beside himself, and a white gleam
glistened in his red eyes; and so discerning,
Satan winged upon the wind, returning
to Uz in quest to ruin the priest
who had begun another day of feast
at his eldest son's home—the holy hem
was soon to unravel—unknown to them
the war to end some lives no one could stem.

CANTO THREE

Stanza 5

The Sabeans came from the south, slaying
servants with long sabers, stealing his stock—
"killing for the sake of it," a slave in shock
cried, who lived to tell of Dark's crusade
before retaliation could be made.
Another wounded servant fell, laying
in blood caused by fire from the sky; green
hillside scorched and corpses spoil'd a still scene,
transformed into a breath of hell—sheep, slaves
strewn, and disfigured, the carnage, in waves
of flames that engulfed the helpless beings.
The servant whispered that God sent the fire.
"No," a voice declared, "Light is not a liar."
"Carnage is the mark of Ares," a slave
shouted, from a corner; "No one could save
anyone; nothing! Death, in its anglings
for men, sink gnarly hooks, three at a time;
horses dragging bodies in mud, and grime;
he's void of feelings just like a demon;
fear-inducing god of every bogeyman."
Job tried to end his rambling to no
avail. "He'd kill with thunderbolts, but
would not overlook so many lives. What
do you think this all came from, master Job?"
Prince of the air knew who controlled the globe;
his army with subtle snares, sets goals to show

souls plagued by pride, and are distrustful.
Dark felt alive with purpose, a willful
challenge, determined to be triumphant—
this time prepared to be the Jubilant.
Dark's plans were operationally good;
experience in every falsehood,
beginning before mankind understood.

Stanza 6

Job put on his old leather warrior
attire, and grabbed his great two-edged
sword, and with haste shouted a heated pledge
to destroy these enemies of life. He
mounted his stallion and charged the mêlée
killing two, then five—by noon, his rapier
had slain murderous Sabeans, offspring
of Saba, offspring of Ishmael, teaching
never worked—death alone answered their hate—
two thousand that morning met their fate.
This son of Issachar had been hated
because of seemingly infinite wealth,
his prowess in battle with poise and stealth,
and his profound love for his family.
Comrades were at his command, steadily
urging him to war. He had created
this predisposition to win crucial
battles, for there had been one primal
goal: no prisoners; they may keep gold, and
silver, to support their adjacent land

to the grand estate of Uz. Job created
pastures, meadows, three wells—a paradise
where, as priest of the Most High, he made precise
thank offerings, and sin offerings for
all throughout Uz, and beyond. He would implore
God, as Light and Love to shed His grace on
everyone as fire, blood, spice, meat, and wood
 mingled as one, an offering that would
more than please Light; it would honor Him, and
His Holy throne as in the days of grand-
father Jacob; not always fond bygone
times, but times when Patriarchs respected
the law of God, yet they had not expected
more of light they were ever protected.

Stanza 7

Without warning, Sabeans were killing
unarmed slaves in a jocular spirit
as though beheading rivals, inspirit
encouraging their forces to attack
without any fear of counterattack;
unarmed people slain in a spine-chilling
manner, hopeless and shocked in this quiet
land—no intelligent way from this riot—
innocent souls choking on blood; the moans
as soul's released final breath; and groans
came from under muffled hoofs again flesh
with unconcern as twisting stallions
trampled, whinnied, rode by rapscallions.

Penetrating shrieks from a murderous
army, some atop camels, thunderous
noise—odor filled cloudy air like horseflesh
or uncooked meat. Suddenly, Job and his
army, who had killed three thousand godless
adversary of Uz, watched the remaining foe
retreating. Bodies everywhere, although
to Job, something was amiss. A flash, then
fire fell from the sky over his son's
home. He cried out, "This is shit. My loved ones
are there." The men had seen Job galloping
off, and followed in haste, and walloping
their horses attempting to catch up. When
they reached the son's home, they heard Job wailing;
they dismounted and stood outside failing
to understand; reasoning on their own;
no one spoke. Unexpectedly, unknown
uneasiness had blown in on a chill-
ing wind, the calm of triumph, the tranquil
sense of these moments passed and yet stood still.

Stanza 8

The soldier held his son; viewed his other
children who had been blackened like little
lambs, over-baked, gone, beyond use, brittle
like burned in an oven. He rose from the
ashes; his son crumbled to the floor, the
man prayed to Light, "Send Michael, or another,
for I will avenge my children with this
Arch Angel's aid." He mounted, blew a kiss,

toward the spirit of his children, and
led the remaining troops toward his grand
hillside home. As they drew nearer, ankle
pain pulled at Job; he saw his wife swaying
side to side as she sat, legs crossed, praying
out loud, screaming, placing blame on Light's Name,
"For God alone could do this--to shoot flame
and fire down to kill my children, rankle
me not." Ocher colored smoke rose above
garden homes; there's an unseen stoker, love
was not behind this heinous crime, he thought,
and he was sure that it was Dark and fraught
to the core—seething with anger—ready
to avenge this diabolical wrong.
His wife, angry and afraid to prolong
war, but he had shaped the lush Land of Uz
and revenge—the pure solution, because
death silenced enemies, and unsteady
or precarious alliances. His
pastoral Eden destroyed, and faith, his
foundation now shaken with doubt and fear
but looking at his wife, motherless, fear-
fulness replaced joy, and Omnipotence
vanished, it seemed for her, "It's impotence
for even angels failed beneficence."

Stanza 9

Job was in a quandary, lost in thought;
sought Light more than any obedient

man could dream. Job had wanted radiant
Guidance and care. He alone—omniscient.
This was why Job had been hated; fate,
that unsure lie, worries men and it aught
not, for a lie is like an infringement
to the psyche, much like Job's maltreatment.
Had not Michael, from the army of Light,
whose blade of righteousness, brought fright
to any foe, taught Job his art of death,
fighting by his side when a thousand died.
Job had once fought beside Michael, but spied
Michael's sword gleaming in sunlight, slicing
through men like they were lard; and enticing
Job to be a valiant mega-death
warrior far above all other men
of war, so if Light created him, then
how could he be wrong as his wife complained.
It was time for action, but unrestrained.
He called his ten commanders for a count
of troop strength; they reported twenty-six
thousand fighting men—ready for the mix
of blood and sweat, pain and glory, many
were from Job's family; a bright sunny
day in May, but men found that it amount-
ed to just another day for honor
in the field of war. These exploits of gore
were not for faint-hearted men; strapping on
leather body protection; where-upon
one saved life is preferred by comrades than
to see a dead relative, friend, or an
enemy striking down any good man.

CANTO FOUR

Stanza 10

*J*osiah was the greatest of Job's ten
commanders; more fierce than twenty soldiers.
From the tribe of Benjamin—ancestors,
small in number, but unusually
strong in battle, and he usually
would fight as though the battle was his, then
lead men into the heated fray, killing
with spear then sword; once—no weapon, unwilling
to quit, he took a club from an rival
and killed him with it; with the arrival
of other armed comrades, he took charge and
won the intense skirmish with no lives lost.
His sword, from heel to point was highly glossed,
and prided himself in wearing the best
 leather shields, all crafted for the finest
dressed soldier in the army. He, a grand
man of men, and he was handsome: dark hair,
nice brown eyes, square jaw, and quite muscular.
Obadiah was second in command,
but what had been said of Josiah, grand
as it was, could also be said of him,
he passionately disliked anyone
who hated Job, and he called him the one
born of Leah, Jashub. He could be kind
at times, if sleeping or if so inclined.
He loved Israel—was from Ephraim

He was just like Josiah, except for
handsome. He was tall and broad, or
wide, and he was never found to rattle
during confrontation in a battle.
No enemy got by him, his shield and
huge sword blocking blows, wheeling, cutting, and
faithfully led men under his command.

Stanza 11

Job summed the commanders and numbered
fighting men—twenty-six thousand readied
for battle. Experienced soldiers he'd
fought beside—many in youth—became friends
to this day. He had other men come, friends
he had made on distant journeys numbered
twelve hundred. Josiah requested to
be heard, as he pushed by commanders to
the front. He paused, then stood up on a large,
bolder in the hillside. "I come to charge
and challenge all who support our hated
Job. I've a great shock, before we embark
concerning this campaign and Patriarch.
Even now look behind you," he pointed,
"The tribes of Israel have appointed
three hundred thousand men have conflated
quickly; they are a murderous nation
from Saba. This assembled formation
of Israelites will devastate the
drunken murderous Sabeans, and the
Land of Uz will be redeemed; Job will

have a garden of peace again—tranquil
lush, and happy. Let's mount, march, fill
our hearts with God's blessing for Light
will honor our efforts, and again fight
our fight." Shouts arise through the ranks. "With skill,"
Obadiah shouted, "we go forth to
crush the evil slayer of children—to
assure victory, our brothers are here
to aid in this war, and we need not fear."
Over three hundred and sixty thousand
men of war organized into ranks, manned
weapons of choice—waited for their command.

Stanza 12

Job led his ten commanders in front of
the other tribes and halted three miles from
Saba, then he sent scouts to spy, wherefrom
the Sabeans originally came.
From Uz, they'd put their wicked foe to shame,
fighting daringly with passion and love
for their Patriarch and for peace, killing
anyone who had resisted, willing
to do what had to be done as soldiers.
Word from the Kingdom of Saba, *butchers,*
someone referred them, finally came
The king had heard what Israel's God had
done in behalf of Job, and the nomad
tribes that surrounded Uz. The leadership
of Job and commanders who's swordsmanship
outstripped the Saba King's best and became

the unsurpassed challenge he had ever
witnessed, and he knew that nothing clever
would work, so he decided to sue for
peace, or a treaty of some kind, before
more havoc, death, and embarrassment had
occurred. He sent an emissary to
Job and the leadership requesting to
set up a meeting to form a treaty.
Worried king hoped that such an entreaty
would not be ignored. Job set the time, had
all principle leaders invited, and
the army readied for the next day, and
prayed to God for guidance. An alliance
consummated only with compliance
to God's will. "We praise Light for his guidance,
for his everlasting love, providence,
power, and might," Job prayed with confidence.

Stanza 13

The King of Saba came out to Job with
a party of twenty-three, and was shocked
at the great army of Job who had blocked
any possible escape: whether to
the east, west, or north, for his back was to
the sea. A treaty was done, and therewith
he signed the document Job had prepared.
Certainly, nothing in common but shared
a sip of wine to seal the deal as tired
king smiled through white gritted teeth mired
in this one-sided agreement like one

in quicksand, death, not far away, paltry
in his own thoughts, he rode back to safety.
Job signaled his troops to assemble as
did all the Israelite tribes, and alas,
the war had ended. The king stood alone
on his balcony and watched their dust rise
into the sky, wondering how unwise
his decision—as more than three hundred
thousand strong men moved away, filled with dread
he retired to his room. The palace
was somber and still. Shouts of Israel
yet be heard in the distance, "Israel,
Israel, God is with us without end..."
Dark stormed into the Celestial, and
marched as though he belonged in this Palace,
demanded an audience with Light—
Michael the Archangel halted; with might,
put sword swiftly under the chin of Dark.
"Pardon dear one, I didn't mean to bark.
I'm here due to a mere discrepancy.
Light did not keep a bargain—errancy
if you will—perchance,—focused fallacy."

Stanza 14

Light transported Dark to his golden throne,
and requested an explanation for
his insolent outburst. "Atten-tion. Your
not to disrespect my Palace." Strangely
Dark, already form straight, noticeably
clicked his heels, feeling painfully alone,

brought his hands to his side, and leveled his
chin. With eyes staring straight, he noticed: *Is
Light silent because of some motive?*, but
he did not dare speak. Michael was at what
seemed, striking distance, then suddenly Light
spoke, "How may I assist you, Dark? At ease."
"My actions were lawful atrocities,
approved by you, so that Job would fail, I
mean, be tested. Instead, you simply defy
your own law; he was permitted with might,
great blessing to destroy my selected
minions, the Sabeans. Job, elected
to serve You, protected by You. Care,
if you will, is all he has known, an heir
to prosperity. He doesn't need to
ask, for blessings fall like spring rain, and who
would think, my god, that such outpouring—new
every day, You have protected this man
outright, no thought for another human—
Predestination? Fate? O my, my, phew,
pardon the theological slip-up—
his eyes turned blood red, lips purple, and fed-up;
his armor made a sizzling sound, it
turned hot; Michael sensed danger as Dark bit
both thin lips. "Now," he began, "shall we come
to some agreement so that I may put a plumb-
line through his soul to validate his sum?"

Stanza 15

Light grinned at Dark's iniquitous scheming,
infuriating Dark again. "Perhaps
overlooking killing ten—a mad lapse
in judgment—or did it simply muddle
your brain? Return to Uz and befuddle
Job, if you are able," Light said, seeming
to conclude the matter, but added, as
Dark began to come to attention, "Crass
malevolence has gained you nothing. Job
now rides into his land with royal robe
draped over his shoulders—conqueror and
priest. Your evil will not influence his
allegiance to me. Dare not kill him. This
is my word." Dark cleared his throat, "I need not
kill him. When I finish with him, he'll blot
you from his mind as though never there, and
curse you until he dies." Dark smirked. Light shouted
"Atten-tion. This priest is mine." Dark doubted
it. "Your insolence is laughable. Get
out of my sight. A liar's tongue, a threat,
a jealousy of some sorts, or depraved
imagination, and I should add, that
a loser stands before me. A Sabbat
of one week, I give to Job, and then you
may inflict him, but whatever you do,
enough killing." Light saw that Dark's face craved
to say something. "At ease," Light nodded to
him. "Well, nothing like tying my hands. You
play a hard game with me with Your humans.

You pick this man because like Eve, women's
psyche will succumb too easily to
me." Light shook his head in disbelief. "You
are filled with foolish, dire gibberish too."

Stanza 16

"Atten-tion. Go from my presence with your
diabolical life," Light shouted which
brought a loud rumbling, at a low pitch
throughout Paradise." At that, Dark was sent
hurling into the cold atmosphere, bent
like a curved bread stick, heading for earth, for
this audience with Light had meant nothing.
His course, firmly set, and this, something
like his chief challenge since Eden. His smile
was broad, leading minions, mile after mile.
They sped and soared over the Land of Uz,
quietly, contemplating what was to
be their next move. "What a marvelous view,"
came from behind Dark. He tried to ignore
it. "This place looks better already, for
we've been gone just weeks." Dark turned, this was
it. "Shut your toothy jaws. Help me with our
plan. Try thinking productively. The hour
is near. Why is it always up to me?"
They swooped down to a gnarled old tree.
"Ah, an old Olive tree. Not much shade though,"
"What the hell do you care about the shade?
Let's get thinking about how we might aid

wonderful Job. I want him to suffer
to the point of death—not death. God's offer
or directive must stand. What I plan to
do is nothing short of miraculous.
We can accomplish this meticulous
undertaking in three parts: first, let him
feel sorry for his loss after grim-
ly speaking with his wife; secondly, bring
excruciating ailments of sting
to his skin. Then have loyal friends mocking…

CANTO FIVE

Stanza 17

*J*ob's surviving servants could not be calmed
nor could the priest conciliate their gloom—
issues too perplexing. In the next room,
his wife wept. She whimpered, "They killed our ten
offspring, and you left me after two weeks, and then
I thought that I'd never see you, this qualm-
ish feeling couldn't be abated. " He
took her hands, fell down to his knees to plea
for forgiveness; quickly his eyes watered.
The father and husband said, "I slaughtered
men to intensely avenge for the loss:
our children—and your injury. Light
knows well my heart, and my impulsive fight
that had been insensitive to your heart.
Will you forgive me? We can now restart
 or revive our love, Kallista. Cosmos
will bless our passion, rekindle the flame
that has been who we are. I feel the same
obsession. No woman has turned my head,
you're the most beautiful by far. I've said
this beyond the Land of Uz, and in all
of my travels." He held her in his arms
and sang softly from his memorized psalms.
She stared at her rings, and sniffled, then wiped
her eyes, but inside, ache, the good life swiped
away like some cosmic fiend had stolen small

sections of her consciousness; hearing but
not, as though in a twilight sleep, but what
could she do; she was in a daze, going
through the motions. The mundane and trifling
duties were like she wasn't there as she
imagined Hades, a sleepless state, he
would not understand. She wanted to flee.

Stanza 18

"I am very happy that mother came
to stay. She is up in our son's destroyed
home, praying to her god. She had enjoyed
the visit, so she said but had clearly
been concerned. Fear of their return nearly
drove us mad. Servants every day became
anxious when they heard thunder or any
peculiar noises. We have had many
rainy days this summer. There were times right
after you left, when in the early night,
the incessant hum of voices—mother
praying out loud, servants chattering, then
imaginary sounds in the house, then
because alone and experienced,
other noises like two goats tied against
the house added to the sounds of others
with their nonstop bleat and baa, all muddled
together nearly made me scream. Huddled
in bed, I prayed to your God for your return." She
gently pulled away and sat down. Yet, he
said nothing, and undressed. Guilt flooded him

with determination like a pilgrim
good and conscientious; Yahweh knew him
well. Job's journey had always included
others, and this duty of love included
in the Law, aided him when choices grim
demanded action. At least he tried; he
needed her; he snuggled his wife as she
was sleeping. He touched her hair, recalling
when they had met on Kittim, rain falling
and the sun trying to shine; she fifteen
and he twenty-six. The island—pristine,
she the most beautiful woman he'd seen.

Stanza 19

When she had awakened, just after dawn,
they ate quietly; her mother, in bed
but awake contemplating gloomy dread.
"Who brought this terror on us? Did someone
sin? I can't believe that children, not one,
deserved death," she kept talking, "you're drawn;
I see the pain of a priest in your eyes,
hear it in your voice, you cannot disguise
fear—not of a warrior—a man, heir
of god. Daily you presented for their
sin, offerings and sacrifices. I
despise all your offerings, they were but
a lie." Job, about to interrupt… "What
can you say, they are dead. Your God is harsh.
They were not evil," she sobbed. "Abash
yourself. One must be humble, Job. Shenai

said that God orders all of life, unlike
other gods." Job insisted, "He is. Strike
that thinking from your mind," as he raised his
right palm at her. "God is God." (Two glasses
and other items flew from the table
as he had forcefully swung across the
surface.) Kallista jumped up pushing the
chair away, and stood there. "God is maker
of all that you have seen, and Creator,
who before time, had spoken, and able,
to craft all living beings, including
humans and angels. Don't be concluding
anything about God based on your Greek
gods. Fate is a pagan's faith, God's unique,
for He is unchangeable in nature.
I want his love, protection, and nurture
for you. I feel the same discomfiture."

CANTO SIX

Stanza 20

Beneath and around the old Olive Tree,
Dark, his lieutenants, and minions had all
assembled. Tatterius, first in charge, tall
and quite vile. Next was Implicatus,
cunning, malicious; all there to discuss
the destiny of Job and the mêlée.
The Dark Prince called his commanders to form
in columns, and in an instant they swarm-
ed like bees, with a whoosh into long rows;
the sound—like that of twenty tornados.
"The upright priest is weakened, and shall soon
be mine. This son of the earth is but flesh
as was all from Adam to Gilgamesh—
sinners created in God's..." his lips burned;
his visage froze; twisted perceptions turned
to the clatter of drawn swords. A triune
voice of holy commanders cried out, "Halt!"
Satan's legions stood down. "The insult,
this blasphemous speech must be admonished,"
said Michael. Like a mute, Satan's anguished
mind couldn't conjure a retort to respond
to archangel's charge. His eyes, black pupils
in narrow pools of red, darted. *Councils,
symbols, archangels—what are they to me?"*
he thought with a hidden smile. "I oversee..."
Light's voice jolted the pause, "We have no bond.

These tested, dauntless spirits once had thrown
you and a third of all hosts from my throne
to your interim realm. Powerless to
me, and my army of angels in lieu
of the fact—your insubordination
thrust you into a lesser manifestation:
lower than archangel's supreme station."

Stanza 21

The breath of Light's anger with potency
shook the air like nature has done with close
lightning, thunder—together; to disclose
power to Dark's army, reminding them
of His might. "Icy veins know naught of men,
for mortal's desire, expectancy,
is to put on immortality. Dark,
your split tongue invites iniquity; mark
my words, you may tempt my anointed, but
you will find him like Noah—true, and what
being like you could fathom a heart like
 mine—a Father's heart. Archangels abhor
blaspheme. Don't rouse their righteous furor.
Carry on, but I can view each move." The
minions let out a sigh, heard Dark yell a
command to come to attention—godlike.
 "Where's Tatterius and Implicatus?"
Quickly the two commanders knelt. "Discuss
with me, just what you two have come up with."
He turned his back to the pair. "I forthwith
declare that I will show Light the measure

of me," he cried out, and made a stiffened
bow. "Perhaps one day I will have riddened
myself of Him. *Lucifer*, Light named me…
no matter," he shrugged. "Enough about me,
for now, it's time to trap this sage. Pleasure
is to rid myself of this battle, this
pressure, this *holy man*—even that is
an true oxymoron," he laughed, but was
angry. He hated theonomy. As
he had often thought, I am a god too.
"I wouldn't be as vile. All is a skew.
What's a misunderstood spirit to do?"

Stanza 22

"This struggle with mankind, from Adam to
Job, is a predicament, that is why
I must remedy it, to regain my
stature; I must defeat Job; shit if I
were such a loser, why is it that I
am here?" He grinned crookedly, "I'll do
as I wish. I rule over legions; have
authority to change my form; have
the strength of more than hundred men—
mighty warriors, I should say. Again,
this falsely accused god," he hits his chest.
"Well enough about me. Tatterius,
what's going on in Uz?" He notices
that Dark is right above him; fear and dread
come over him. "Master we have," he said,
facts that Job's wife is not quite at her best,

and that his mother-in-law serves Greek gods
and that she frequently says that Job's odds
with one God are far from reality."
Dark 's patience had waned, "Triviality,
you insignificant fool." "But Master…"
"Shut up. Stand up." Implicatus then said,
"Job is questioning why God let this dread
come upon him and his wife," he spoke in
fear, rattling off his tale. "To begin
with, this is better. First-rate disaster
to the soul has its genesis in poor
weakened souls. My, this is fertile ground, or
should I say major territory for
temptation. I see light out there before
me. I feel that former trials fade
as hope grows within. I am not afraid;
I should be; as for me—can't be remade."

Stanza 23

"I am sending you both back to Uz to
Job's self-important friends to acquire their
skewed opinion of him. I know that there
will be gossip. Man, unintentionally
fabricates, twists truth. Eventually
I will triumph," he added pointing to
his commanders with his index finger.
"I will find myself in, calm my anger."
Dark moved about, then with hands behind his
back, strolled in a large circle. "This is
folly to some who are but trembling fools.

Didn't I win in Eden?" "But Master,
the Covenant…" Satan grimaced. "No Master!"
Evil One's finger nails were thrust into
the large imp's neck and groin; threw him onto
a burning altar. "Don't forget who rules
you insubordinate ass. We're at war."
"My Eminence, these flames; mercy, no more."
He pushed Implicatus from the fire.
"Perhaps being busted to your prior
rank would curb your foul interjections. Fools,
I took one-third of the angels, and got
numbskulls. I refuse to lose and then rot
in hell." He shook his head in disgust. "Why
is it so difficult for you?" A sigh,
 "So much is at stake in this quest. Our tools
for war must include cunning, so vile
this mortal will beg for some relief while
cursing life." Dark was getting excited.
He believed that all had been united.
"Job's special offerings will not smell sweet,
if you and your companies truly mete
out punishment after each holy feat."

Stanza 24

*D*ark adjusts his black armor and breathes
deeply. "Humans are an experiment;
logic confirms this painful argument.
"So easily does envy seduce them,"
said Tatterius. "We must not condemn
their trinkets of gold; the honor of wreathes

put on the heads of kings or men of letters.
Many have sighed, pinched by their own fetters."
They smiles in unison, but all were hushed
by a curiously faint sound. Dark brushed
by two; stopped, "Listen," as he unsheathes
his sword quicker than light, "we're not alone."
Strangely, altar flames began to be blown,
feverishly lapping at the gray air.
Not one of them did anything but stare
like mannequins, frozen in thought, not fear.
Dark opined, "Damnation? Endless morning?
Is not judgment preceded by warning?
Light's laws are immutable, or are they?
Obviously, the thing has veered away."
All at once a massive brilliance so queer
zoomed by the south entry: short, sharp, shrilling;
sounds: rattling, shaking—calm. "Sniveling
cowards," said Dark, swatting Tatterius
with the side of his blade. "Get up. Piteous
fool. Whatever it was, it's gone." His sneer
tightened the coward's throat, but not his wit;
"I suppose, my lord, I'm but a nitwit,
yet my fealty is thoroughly to you."
He bowed before his sire sitting, who
brooded. Tatterius, with a careful eye,
withdrew; the silent throne did not reply.
The pair stood at ease; exhaled a still sigh.

Stanza 25

Lucifer's squinted red eyes were fixed in
deliberation; his nails tapped his throne
in annoying rhythm; vengeance planned bone-
chilling nights for the shepherd-priest in Uz,
but also retaliation because
this time he would outsmart Light—no chagrin.
A commotion, loud echoes of chatter;
Checked his contemplation, "What's the matter
now?" he barked. "Implicatus, please," one eye
closing in disgust, "stop that clatter. Why
such incompetence? Training. Discipline.
Decorum. But then, quite providentially,
I don't tire" Looks at his mug, sips raki,
his own concoction. He sets down the cup
and watches the noisy troop approach. "Up,
up you buffoon. Jezbez quickly stands.
"Sir, Airlie returns from Uz to report
a potent battle, Light's direct support
of Job, and Michael's mission that had made
a win hopeless; his unforeseen blockade—
impregnable. Airlie misunderstands
this decisive defeat." "Enough. Let him speak."
Airlie bows. "Rise. You were dauntless. This sneak
attack will be addressed when I account
to Light. No. No, rather, when I recount
all these grievances. Look at your armbands.
Even your armor is charred." Dark places
his hands on Airlie's arms, then embraces

him—benevolent master to loyal
servant—soldier to soldier. The Royal
Prince of Darkness knows well that war is hell.
Airlie tells how the Archangel's wrath fell
protecting the priest in his lonely dell.

Stanza 26

"Why would the Sabeans attack again?
They have a damn treaty with Job from the
last war; they had to high-tail it, back the
way they had come—to Saba. Answer me."
Tatterius explained, "This new melee,
with about five hundred warriors, and
a few chariots, which came from the east,
not Saba." "How, on this globe, could that priest
amass an army?" "He didn't, Light fought
for him." "What! That's wrong. I'm fraught
with disgust." He sprang up. "Light's disregard
for rules of war. At least, in this instance,
this clash shouldn't be—misalliance,
but rather to my advantage. We split
on the Uz attack: I killed humans, spit,
I confess, and animals—with regard
to sacrifices of some sort, there were
a few who were unblemished entrants, per
the Law, for blood offerings. Humph, never
thought of that. But then again, whatever.
Look, Light saved Job and his wife. Oh, and two
servants. Fair is fair, but using Michael

and his army was unfair. Mystical
beings get on my nerves. In fact, he is
the one who threw us out. They are asses.
Just forget it Tatterius, this too,
upsets you. Let's refocus on the priest."
He clenched his left fist, lifting it, "At least
the war can still be won," he smiled, this
time showing sharp white teeth, then, lifting his
chin revealed his purple lips tightly etched
against the back of his throne. He stretched,
"My goal to win is not that far-fetched."

CANTO SEVEN

Stanza 27

Job's lush land, barns, and home were repaired or
completely rebuilt. Workman: carpenters
who had labored the longest; stonecutters
and masons all spent months on the project.
Job kept busy; his wife did not expect
Uz to ever be the same lush place, nor
could she forgive Light, Job, or her mother's
many gods. The friends of Job and others
attempted to dissuade her by saying that
the murder of her ten children, whereat
was not by spirits, it was the evil,
drunken vagabonds who had a free will.
Kallista would shake her head, and say, "Still
you pester me with theories, after all;
just go away. These assumptions are all
you offer. Go away." Job's unsure will
wavered at times when he heard people say
these things to her. He couldn't find a way
to refute this dilemma, and so said
nothing. Lately, not feeling well, he said
to a friend that he had a hard time in
the early morning getting out of bed,
and in the afternoon, felt that his head
throbbed when in the hot sun; his legs ached
and sharp pain caused sweats. Once he had quaked
as false fear came over him; his dry skin

itched "probably from fighting wars most
of my life," he'd say. Revealing the ghost
in a recurring dream had never been
mentioned. "I'm thirty-six, so tell me when
the real pain will begin," he said to
Benai, his friend, also a priest. "To do
all that you have done—I honor you."

Stanza 28

In Uz, the quiet seemed unnerving.
There were smoldering burning places where
fires had been set to burn trash from where
the original home of Job and his
lovely Kallista had once stood, and this
is where the only well that was serving
the occupants of Uz; the other three
wells had been polluted, and were to be
cleaned or new ones dug. The fifth month had seen
much accomplished to bring back a pristine
appearance, a sense of normalcy, one
thing that made him feel good was to get up
to sunlight—not smoke that was so close-up
that you could taste it. He gathered wood for
a Thanksgiving Offering; done before,
 many times, for blessings God had outdone
in his behalf, based on Melchizedec's
book. Job's clean heart had no presumptuous
attitude. Kallista refused the meal.
Job ate alone; wondering what would heal
her broken heart. *Would God make her whole*, he

questioned, for he really understood her;
recognized her anguish; and wanted her
to hold him, but she would have nothing to
do with him, and he perceived—she too
was lonely, not just aloof. Often, he
had not considered her opinion in
what he was about to do, for his in-
cite or vision was paramount: priest,
soldier, shepherd—none presented the least
difference—Job's traditions, not the man.
His heart was in the right place—no one can
fault him for that--he's a partisan.

Stanza 29

*J*ob sat under a Sycamore tree one
crisp break of day, thinking about how he
often had been blessed in battle; for he
had seen a glowing sword swinging, flashing,
killing the enemy—like the cracking
lightning; his holy steel preserving one
battle at a time to protect a man
of God in war. It was Michael, for man-
kind, *probably in all wars of righteous-
ness over evil* Job thought. This, a joyous
thought put a smile on him as he gazed at
the cloudless sky. He was reassured that
Light had always fought for him, never at
his back, but leading the way to conquest
through His Archangel Michael—utter best
of angels. This had been revealed at

Saba; Job was gazing at the city.
"The Gray Angel of Death will kill only
if needed for a rout of the rival
unrighteous." He felt the sense: *revival*
as he breathed in the early morning air.
The aches and discomfort of warrior
days abated. He thought, *interior
northeast of the Land of Uz needs some work;*
work he had done with sons in fall—fieldwork.
The laughter, sweat, and closeness of each heir.
He gathered some tools, threw them in a cart;
asked two servants to help; this: a restart
of good. He looked toward the house, again
felt the sting of loss: ten offspring, again,
a sorrowful wife. *Would to God that He
restore my loss* he sighed; looked up at the lea
moved toward it. *Life—there's no guarantee.*

Stanza 30

*I*n his youth, he sailed the Great Sea along its
northwestern coast of Kittim where he found
his teenage wife, Kallista. Renowned
was her family in Kittim; but his
wealth opened arms and concessions; riches
always brought him more. In-laws liked what its
influence, power, and glitz afforded
them. Kallista's many gods were recorded
on trinkets and jewelry she wore, or
icons shelved or hung; but her beauty bore
fame in the tiny city-state, for it's

she who was God's idea of beauty
in Job's mind, for she singly, a beauty
in any man's mind, youthful and refined.
A flower most perfect and shy, and kind.
Job spent six month in the city, but credits
her good father for betrothing her to
him, expressing to them happiness to
eternity. She had a fine dowry,
but they had to marry in the cirque
on the mountain side, near the sea with green
grass everywhere at that time of year;
it was as soft as a temple rug. "We're
glad you have agreed to this location.
Our families have wed here; our elation
is obvious I'm sure." It was a lovely scene
for such a handsome couple. The prayer
from a Greek priest caught Job quite unaware;
Benai, Job's priest friend, could not understand
the insinuation of the grandstand;
it praised Zeus and lesser strange gods that shocked
Job, for Kallista had bewitched and rocked
her husband; his friend who felt just as mocked.

Stanza 31

The God of Job's religion was surely
patient with people who worshiped Him and
other gods; constraints of free will demand
certain latitudinal limits on mankind
that often put priests, like Job, in a kind
of quandary. The response was holy;

God is Holy, so worship Him thusly
in Holiness. Reality: justly
work with fallen man who says one thing, tries
to do it, but fails; without warning dies—
usually. Job believed in Heaven.
Kallista felt misunderstood; Job sought
to help by explaining how she ought
to follow monotheism, and then
everything would be fine, in fact when
they returned to Uz, for she would even
find it lush, green, peaceful, a place to love
life, raise children and grandchildren to love.
She listened to Job before the wedding
seemingly as though he had been shedding
light on her paganism, a form of
idolatry; they: manmade gods, above
all, sterile icons of deception; love
an emotion void in stone and clay, known
only by their human creator; shown
to be deaf, similar to the ears of
Kallista's behavior at the service
backfired, caused consternation, nervous
family was speechless, thought it serious;
in fact, it caused a lackluster ruckus.
The ceremony and celebration
concluded, she'd had no hesitation
to address her pagan adoration.

CANTO EIGHT

Stanza 32

"The time has come, *Skin for Skin,* I call it,
just as sure as I had said it to Light.
Pain is something man recognizes; fight,
he will, but man has a limit; a sure
critical point—this is where we'll… Ha! Pure,
poor Job," he grinned. "Anyway, oh shit,
I almost forgot. Me forgetting—not.
Get real. I remember now, we're not
to withhold misery of any sort,
short of death. Do not defy me, purport
to justify failure, or any such
nonsense. I find great pleasure in war, much
like at Eden." Head snapped around; such
speed; such hate; looking for Implicatus.
"Should any imp abort duty to us,
I mean me; that regretful imp shall touch
death sooner than revelation proposed.
Pull out the stops, pain everywhere supposed
to come from Light. His aged martial body
will wither like an old man; nobody
will be able to aid him—wife, healers,
friends, not even Light. I will break him down."
Dark was in his glory tonight; showdown
was about to happen. Officers and
imps celebrated; armor polished; with grand
red armbands around each arm, they're dealers

of death for the final battle. Our theme
will be *Skin to Skin* for soon the dull scream
in the night from Uz as the priest writhes in
unquenchable pain, believing soon, sin
is the cause. There's no remedy to be
found; lost just as a shipwrecked man at sea;
wife and friends will quickly tire—let him be.

Stanza 33

"Before I make my move on Job, let us
visit his friends, Eliphaz, Bildad, and
Zophar. Find weaknesses; study close and
look for defects of character that we
will use against Job. You know the drill: we
tempt their craving or desire; don't fuss
with passive wants; then, offer them what
they wish—with beneficial conclusions, but
make sure they are solid offerings for
the unsuspecting prey, make sure before
you tempt these humans, as I did to Eve,
Samson, and many like them in between:
capeesh?" "Huh?" asked Airlie. "Oh boy. I've seen
this happen many times; you fowl up. Fool,
temptation is the first step; make them drool
for their envied or covetous want; leave
a vision of this, and mark it in their
craniums—with a positive end." There
you've got him! Snap!" He clicked his long fingers.
"The completed result—hurt that lingers.

Do you get it? Airlie, never mind, stick
with Decepticus. You are too lazy,
thick in the middle. Some imps are crazy,"
he said to himself. "I am furious
inside," he gasped to Tatterius.
"This is not meant to be some foolish trick.
I'm looking ahead to a better day
out there," he pointed toward the pathway
that led to the Celestial. "Never
mind," he shuddered. "I'm clever.
I know, sentimentality is not
me, yet, I didn't get my region—not squat,
because I had been brighter than the lot."

Stanza 34

"Let me explain. I had free will. I had
been the most intelligent, yes, the most
intelligent—with free will. I don't boast,
perhaps sometimes; nevertheless, think on
this: a third of the holy army—one
at a time, ok, many more imps had
left with me. I must admit, Light out shined
me; Ha, yah get it. Light had out *divined*
me. Anyway, enough about what was,
or will be," he complained—then shivered as
though his rambling had bothered him. "What's
the matter with me?" he said angrily.
At a distance, running toward him—Airlie.
He looked weary, nearly wobbling, flush;

"Airlie! Why are you here? What is the rush?
Whoa, too many questions." Airlie gasped. "What's
the matter? Why were you running?" "Because
you said that I needed," he swallowed, "cause
I had to shrink my middle." "Ha, ha, ha,
ha, ha, you are hilarious. Pooh-Bah,
that's how I would classify you. Where is
Decepticus?" "He's coming," said Airlie.
Dark, frustrated, looked, "My who do I see,"
as Decepticus entered Dark's throne zone.
Dark listened vigilantly to his tone.
"May I speak Master?" Dark nodded twice. "Is
all going as intended?" asked Dark.
"Job's three friends are a symbol, a hallmark
of arrogance, but defend Job as friend.
Praise of him, and loyalty has no end."
"Therefore, we tap into their arrogance;
subtle flaw: masked: more intelligence
than Job; they'll condemn him by inference."

Stanza 35

"Go attack Job. I expect that you will
keep an eye on his three friends as well. Do
as I have taught. Don't delay, time hereto
is short. I'll be waiting for your reports.
If anyone of you fail, misreports,
or any other misconduct, I will
see to it that you are severely dealt
with. Got it?" He looked at the four, felt

a bit reflective, then snapped out of it.
The only regretfulness he had, it
had been long before humans existed.
*Phew, too much thinking bothers me, in fact,
I'm annoyed at myself,* he thought, retract-
ing it, but could not. He swooped down to
Uz to check on the four, and much to
his surprise, Decepticus had twisted
the thinking of Elihu; Airlie had
done the same to Bildad; "What the… egad,"
he said vocally, but caught himself: there
was a chief imp, Implicatus, midair
still attempting to persuade Eliphaz,
that arrogance was simple being self-
assured. Tatterius, ever himself,
self-possessed—such a quality! He
had begun tormenting Job; "appointee
I was pleased to employ; he's as
despicable as me. Ah yes, I see
the disease appearing, didn't foresee
how it was to begin in this soldier,
but, I am pleased, the sores have moisture;
his face grimaces. How quickly they had
appeared. Wife strips clothes; he lies back unclad;
I'm delighted; ecstatic —more to add."

CANTO NINE

Stanza 36

My endmost nemesis is death, Job thought
as he shuffled alone in his enigma.
He passed by lowered heads to his stigma
as powder-like dust puffed around his feet.
Nothing could assuage his grief; sweat from heat
clung to open wounds; he shivered; distraught
as voices from days past echoed when he
entered his disordered house; he could see
their kind faces moving about the room;
he limped by them, approached the backroom.
He sat on his unmade bed and soon caught
the sight of his wife. Tears mingle with pus
and blood fell between his feet; "I loved us,"
he said as she left their room. He awoke
before dawn, ate hard bread, grabbed his cloak
hung torn, another sign or the onslaught
to loss. Painful resting denied much sleep;
prayer: raspy audible sighs, and sheep
of his flock now scattered or stolen.
Petitioning God for help through swollen
lips eased discomfort, for supplication
had once been second nature. Disgrace
and ill-repute were foreign to him. Grace
from Light, made life a joy with family,
friends, and the Land of Uz; security
that made his existence an adulation

to God. He poked with stick at things
he had never noticed before; like rings
around a broken tree, fallen branches,
and pieces of charred wood. Color blanches
in his skin, as pain began down his arms.
Wounds robbed both sleep and judgment, like qualms,
constant misgivings within; nothing calms.

Stanza 37

Job had a better day, not without pain;
he had shaved his head, bathed, combed his beard,
dressed in ceremonial garments; peered
out the sunlit window that morning; wiped
the tears from aches and joy. His striped
robe hung on a dowel; it struck a vein;
his heart was not in any of it, for
his wife had tailored it, the one chore
without excuses, sewn with love; but that
was not the only cause of grief, there at
the top of sorrow's grim ledger, stately
stood priestly, patriarchal positions,
and this would be his last grain apportions
offering for sin because his body
was deteriorating; a shoddy
man is unfit like an imperfectly
offered animal. Elihu said, and
so did others, "perchance a reprimand
is the main reason for your agony
and chiefly due to your sanctimony."

He lifted off his turban, and removed
his robe. Anguish, within, without, again
on his bed undressed, head hung, "Amen."
So be it to all of the accusers;
my spouse, one of the awful abusers,
he thought—*accusations unproved.*
"Good morning Kallista," spoken softly
with weak voice; often felt unworthily.
Kallista, caught off guard, her mind elsewhere,
"Good morning," she said in Greek. "Do you care
for something to eat?" she asked in almost
a monotone. She leaned on the bedpost;
felt older than her age—"I am a ghost."

Stanza 38

*J*ob convinced himself that *maybe I'm wrong,*
he surmised; made his way to table.
Neither spoke; then she said, "Others label
you as a sinner." He didn't answer,
but stared at her: she needed no enhancer
for her beauty—inviting like a song;
mother of ten; smooth radiant skin, men
often found her alluring, but knew when
to leave the Greek heiress alone. She peered
out the window—sons and daughters cheered
on by their father, many years ago.
The recollection of daughters, doting,
on them with a mother's love denoting
a genuine care that was to last far
beyond her living. Now gone, and the scar,

the loss—unbearable. The bright window
reflected the sun. She turned to look
at Job. He—asleep on crossed arms—she shook
it off, left the room with her own feelings.
The situation puzzled her—meanings
of Light's silence, Job's backsliding, disease,
and financial ruin. She stood at the
front door; tears burst from tired eyes; the
joy of life had vanished as fast a Job's
illness. Lost in depression; "Light! Cure Job's
ungodly condition—unknown disease."
That night Job, lying in bed began his
evening prayer: "Man born of woman is
destined to days full of trouble among
any tribe; and goes to a land of long
nights of gloom; we cannot fathom; light
is but a shade of darkness, the dim sight
hinders no one—I'm persuaded by Light."

Stanza 39

Kallista went to Job, who often begs
for her to remain calm as possible;
he worried that it was not implausible
to assume—she might leave, but there
wasn't a real sign for conjecture;
except for a letter that mentions plagues,
punishments, and sins against gods, she had
received from her mother from Kittim; had
Job not seen it on the table, he may
not have had suspicion. It was a grey

day, Job more ill, Kallista more forlorn.
"Yes Kallista," he said. "I think that you
should curse your God. There is no sin. I do
not know why a good man should undergo
such agony, still serve such a God—go
on praying to the wall." She went outside.
He sat quietly; years ago he'd sworn
allegiance and devotion to Light
as soldier and priest, and for either, fight
with all the strength, though little, to the death.
"My Defender and Rock lives; my last breath
will be to serve Him. In my flesh, I will
see God; my heart longs for that day. I'll fill
my mind with these thoughts, O Light, and thrill
at the hope of my Redeemer." He grew
tired and went to rest on his bed. He knew
that one day soon, this life of utter uphill
struggle would end: like questions of illness,
his wife's despair and blame, of the joyless
times that encompass him. He heard chatter;
listened; it was Kallista; *What's the matter?*
he thought. "Brech Elohim vamuth." He
closed his eyes. "I'll not curse God and die. She
is wrong. Light, how did this all come to be?"

Stanza 40

Kallista, alone under a blue sky,
fifty yards from their dreary domicile;
away from everyone, not just Job, while
intermittently, recalling dark smoke

over her childrens homes; then, pulled her cloak
tightly across her breast, how they would cry
even when she would sing to them in Greek,
or at times, Hebrew; brushed tears from her cheek.
She sat against a stone, folded her arms,
looked at the tiny silver trinkets—charms
brought from Kittim replicas of idols,
her father had presented to her, a
holiday gift when twelve with great hoopla.
The wristlet was thought to be jewelry by
Job—saw beauty, not religion; his eye
caught her striking gorgeousness—not idols.
Her charisma also had allured him,
like an inquisitive sheep, young and trim,
handsome, self-assured, he followed her through
the market where idols large and small drew
attention to shoppers. He followed her
until he had bumped into her father
with whom he had been trading goods, further
more he had never met Kallista; they
were introduced. On the trip back, they
shared future plans openly, but not her
idols. She was only fifteen; he ten
years older; it didn't matter, for when
he was with her, he felt youthful, strong;
that was good for a man of war. As long
his days of soldiering were behind him.
He cared for her, but more about the vim
he felt; was not insensitive nor grim.

CANTO TEN

Stanza 41

"I am so good. She's on my side. Truly,
I understand her: Uz, Eden, places
similar, but never the same faces.
Suggestion: the key in temptation, my
how things don't change, keep the humans lying
to themselves to acquire wants, surely
through any ill-gotten method, depraved
they want more. They are never behaved
although some try. An easy mark: she's young,
older ailing husband, fame gone—now unsung,
as hero. I am beside myself—not.
Even poor Job—get it, *poor.*" Imp quartet
did their unison laugh. He is beset,
puzzled about his wife's confusion; the
dire affair has her doubting faith; the
backsliding is a wonderment to him; got
his brain cooking: *the whys:* why me? why God?
and so on. Humans are good at doubt. Prod
them, and they invent more inquiry;
down to the quick sand of a miry
end. It's time to turn the screws and take heart
in our campaign: *Skin to Skin,* as I
had said to Light. Catchy isn't it? I
enjoy coming up with zingers. I'm good
at many things. This Adversary would
fail if this were not a fact. Let's kick-start

this program into high gear," Dark said with
excitement. "I am close, just a hair's breadth,
and I will be free," exclaimed Dark. Four
imp commanders stood with mouths opened, for
this was news to them. Tatterius said, "I'm afraid
I do not grasp the word *free*. An upgrade
of some sort." Dark's contracted face turned jade.

Stanza 42

"*I* will explain at the appropriate
time…" Airlie interjected, "That is a
curious word, so what…" "My god, what a
consummate idiot. Are you deaf as
well as fat? Phew, let me back up; I was
about to say how we will appreciate
being *free* to bring Job to the brink of
death at which time his agony will, of
course, be so intense that he will curse Light
and die." Dark hoped that the quartet—not bright;
bought his explanation of *free*; he knew
what he had meant or desired, but that
was none of their business really, that
had been their downfall eons ago—
misguided allegiance. "You four know
that we have an ally—Kallista. Blue
eyed, quiet beauty, a twenty-nine year
old, with frailties, is able to steer
Job into failure. Be advised, I
will see to it that she bends the reed by
nagging sympathetically and screw

with his head until the combination—
illness and mental strain, short duration,
create the inclination to cry out
the evil prayer to God and die. No doubt,
she'll be engaged to our benefit to
eschew the patriarch until his death.
I can hardly wait to hear his last breath.
A fantastic plan! One variation:
I'll bring endless dissociation
to both spouses, day and night without end,
through persistent thoughts and dreams. I will send
Tatterius to aid. I'll not amend.

Stanza 43

"Campaign *Skin to Skin* will be to seduce
Kallista—the usual persuading:
friendliness, effortless masquerading,
various flirtations, playful touching,
and showing interest by entering
inappropriately her space, to use
any essential meaningful way to
manipulate her for an embrace through
these techniques not necessarily in
that order. Tatterius and I, in
synchronization will work against Job
to add jealousy, self-loathing, to probe
the depth of despair; until frontal lobe
pounds. To top it off, we shall influence
Commander Josiah; self-confidence
is his hallmark; and is the friend of Job.

Josiah will seduce Kallista; he
had continuously considered—she
had been the most beautiful, loving, and
kind woman he had met in any land.
Because of her wealth, refined, and because
she was married, off limits; and a lost
cause—she was Job's spouse, and the dreadful cost
would be grave. He had kept this to himself,
even after his wife's death; lost himself
in a new war in Israel, because
he had been a warrior his entire
life." Airlie said, "So that means that…" Dark's ire
explodes, "Unreal, yikes stupidity;
a mindless, dimwitted imp—oddity."
Airlie's mouth dropped open and remained
so. Dark looked at the others, who remained
at ease; soon Dark's irritation had waned.

Stanza 44

*D*ecepticus continued to work on
the arrogance of Elihu, who was
elevating himself above Job as
he explained the philosophical
nature of sin—made it applicable
to Job's suffering. Elihu said on
more than one occasion that Job had not
been thinking clearly, although this did not
sit well with the Patriarch. Airlie had been
attacking Bildad, for conceit had been
outrageous and prideful. He said to the

priest, "Authority and admiration
belong to Light—no collaboration…
can His forces be numbered? No man can
be righteous; man is but a worm. The span
of the heavens cannot be measured." A
self appointed authority cleared
his throat. Dark told Airlie that he smeared
Job's claims with the truth, permeated with
smugness. "Thank you Master," Airlie said with
a smile. Dark smiled back, and turned to
the next imp, Implicatus, who said, "As
far as it goes with Eliphaz, he was
extremely self-righteous. He said, 'Can man
profit from Light? Would Light gain from a man…
it's because of your piety, that you
create impiety, and Light brings this
agony upon you.' Eliphaz, less
truthful than I've seen in years, goes on to
falsely accuse the priest of being too
greedy. He says that Job, the land owner
with great wealth, yet by no means a donor;
slighted widows and orphans—holy loner."

Stanza 45

"Eliphaz went from philosophy to
utter falsehood. Habitual liar.
That's why I like him," said Dark. "Admire
him, I do. Thus far, Job feels just like
crap in his condition—useless crap. Strike
him more vigorously, and this time to

the bone; I will break his human spirit
like a twig." "Who influenced Zophar? It
seems to me that he is overlooked,"
said Airlie. "He was not overlooked,
minion, for he spewed forth condemnation
pure and direct at the priest. He solely
brought as much as we could on the holy
priest. I could not have expected more from
any of you. This friend of Job's came from
nowhere to give us support. Frustration
is that humans like to blame us for their
sins—not so. Tatterius is in air
on return flight from battering the priest."
Standing in front of Dark, like a black beast,
because of his shiny black armor, was
Tatterius at attention. Dark as
only he could feel: in charge, badass,
everything under his control, lifted
his hand to salute a crisp uplifted
right arm with perfect figure, and he was
grinning with bright white teeth; moist, deep red eyes,
and armor the envy of evil spies.
"Tatterius, you have out done yourself.
Anguish in mind, soul, and body. His self-
worth is an abnormal aberration;
his friends are now an abomination;
 no self-esteem—Oh my—the vexation."

Stanza 46

"Josiah is at home. He had been on
an advice-giving consultation for
battles in the territory of Dor.
Let's enter his house; help him find the small
gold idol that is in the left sidewall,
in the back room. This is the small icon
he had lost years ago. It is the idol that
Kallista had given him; caveat:
he would have to remember her as a
friend," whispered Dark. "Oh shit, if it's not a
piece of gold," Josiah said as he leaned
himself behind the bed to the corner;
tilted down to pick it up, no sooner
had he had it in his hand, "What the hell?
This is the piece of gold I lost," it fell
with a thud to the wood floor, careened
to a bed leg. *This was from Kallista.
How lucky is Job*, he thought. The vista
outside was cloudy, just like his life, for
he was lonely without a woman; war
had taken her place; sometimes a woman
who were paid for, but both made him feel
like stormy days. A thought of Job came: he'll
get things packed; go visit him in Uz.
What's making him think of Kallista? Was
it the idol? Or was it the woman?
He packed for the two week journey; left
with some odd expectation; felt bereft,
and wondered why. His former commander

would see each: officer to commander;
but they had fought side by side, man to man,
for soldiers are brothers; fought from Beshan
to Saba; many more; Job's a man's man.

Stanza 47

"In two weeks, Kallista must look like a
healthy, beautiful, twenty-nine year old;
ripe for Josiah; mix in the four-fold
allures: lusty eye staring, immoral
teasing, lustful enticing; liberal
time together," said Dark with his grin, a
a nasty, toothy, crooked smile. "Heard that,"
said Implicatus in agreement. At
that, Dark said, "I'll get to work on her now,
for she needs a real make over. Wow,
this will be fun; she will be ready—in
a week. *Skin to Skin* program is in fact,
beginning. Tatterius give no slack,
turn the screws tighter on Job—short of death.
One soul lost multiplies to mega-death;
all begging for forgiveness to Light, in
unison, blaming me for their troubles.
Their condition—permanent. These rebels
blame me. So will Kallista after I
play with her emotions. She will think, *"My,*
I wish I'd stayed In Kittim; why did this
tragedy happen to me? Somehow, his
heartbreak tears me from head to toe; this is
not right. What did I do so wrong? I'm

*young; still have my looks—for what? There's no rhyme
or reason; but to worry for a piss
poor dying man. Every day just like before;
vanished in the sunlight; and furthermore…"*
"Whiny humans. Perfect for me. Oh how
They despise working on their problems—Wow,
nothing new. When they're feeling sorry
for their status—fallen, in creeps worry;
helpless to pity—short of mastery."

Stanza 48

"War is shocking, but I don't mind gruesome
killing—humans are adamant—they are
bent on such slaughter; generations are
ever selfishly practicing, but they
never get it right. Our war is way
different with Light—I will overcome
because I am playing fair, following
the set of laws, and Light likes them; showing
restraint is best. Now, where was I? Oh,
I'm going to persuade Kallista; know
this: I don't have to spare her precious life.
I will speak with the Angel of Death, he's
well educated in matters like these;
without delay, ready with a brigade;
each convinced to kill like a renegade.
I could kill Job, if rules were not set; wife…
Hold on. Being paged by Light. Oh my.
There's trouble in heaven; I must draw nigh.
I'll return soon," said Dark. *Whoosh*

An Epic of Job, The Biblical Warrior-Priest

"Dark. What is this I hear of an ambush
on Kallista?" asked Light. "What in g..., oops.
No, I'm appraising options. I mean I
am..." Light interrupted him, "Silence, I
want you to stick to the rules: Harm priest—
not kill him. Use friends against him; at least,
the Angel of Death cannot join your troops
nor be used in any tactic; no overwhelming—
unless I permit. You are performing
beyond these rules and stipulations."
"How do you figure? Your regulations
are not overstepped; rules have not
been broken; this is poppycock, not
factual; except the death cherub rot."

Stanza 49

*D*ark' attitude had began to worsen;
glaring eyes simmered in red pools; a nail
scratched itching neck; just about to wail
to scream something that he might regret, when
swiftly, as though sensing an eruption
of contempt, Michael held that a lesson
was required; his drawn sword cut the air;
he lunged forward; "Watch your tongue, or prepare
to defend your actions," he warned. Light said,
"Dark this is absurd, being a hothead
gets us nowhere; I simply called you to
clarify tactics; to assist you in
a sense." Dark's demeanor calmed, and in
response said, *"Cooperative* is not in my

nature, unless it's one sided—mine, *sigh*,
but I'm trying to adjust it; to do
 better." Light said, "I understand. You are
dismissed." Dark swooped down, descending far
above Uz; saw Kallista; and he felt
good. *I dislike certain words, I've been dealt:
Satan, Dark, Lucifer—adversary
of Light. Once not so*, he thought, looking in
on Kallista. She wore charms, fine linen;
deeply staring in the mirror crying;
felt that all had been lost; felt like dying.
She stood up; opened her robe. Contrary
to her age, motherhood, sorrow—body
was fine. Dressed, perfumed—nobody
would notice; yet today, she wore earrings,
a gold bracelet that was deeply endearing,
from her father, then sensed a better
day. Dark grinned, liked it all—had let her
awaken in a good mood—to tempt her.

Stanza 50

*D*ark had seen that Josiah was about
an hour away. He bombarded her
with good thoughts, after all, as Lucifer,
he was an Angel of Light, even his
inferior imps could masquerade this
kind of deception; Dark had been devout,
and once had been the Morning Star. Dark has
been deceiving humans ever since, as
stories enlarged and spread of the first

lost war against Light, just after the worst
came as he and his minions had been cast
from living in the Golden Palace of
Light, known to angels, and few men, as Love.
"Look at that woman, and here at her door
is Josiah." The knock at the door, more
than anything, frightened her, for past
friends did not visit any more. "Who would
have believed it. Josiah!" She could
not but notice how trim and fit; striking
and tall; she had adorned herself, liking
the way it felt again. "Kallista," he
said, "May I come in?" She opened the door.
He said, "You look good today. How is your
fine husband, Job, my former commander?
Heard that he was ill. I'm no bystander
when it comes to former warriors. He
was rough but fair. My life has been spent in
the army. What kind of shape is Job in?"
"He's with his brothers in the north pasture,
his sons are buried in a sepulcher
near there. Brothers had taken him, so he
could get into the wagon," Kallista
said, then asked Josiah if he'd like a
drink of water. "Will Job return today?"
I've been alone a day; I couldn't say,
for he has been gone up to three days, so
I am not sure." He turned to the door, "Whoa,
I could sleep in his arsenal depot."

DAVID BEN FOSTER

Stanza 51

"This is a good start," said Dark to cohort
Tatterius. "Wait, I'm working on a
little intimacy." Then Kallista
asked Josiah to dinner, and he
smiled, agreed unequivocally,
"How does a man ever turn down disport
with a beautiful woman." It made her
feel quite good. Dark said, "To consider
 this entertainment, it's a fond recall
that he has remembered—her beauty." All
at once, Dark gets word that Job will be back
in the late morning. Before Josiah
goes off to his sleeping quarters, he saw
an opportunity to have a talk
with Kallista—she talked, then she'd walk
around nervously; there seemed a lack
of concentration on Josiah's part;
the way he was staring at her, apart
from unconsciously agreeing with her;
she sensed it, wished to touch him, but neither
did anything inappropriate. He
stood up and said, "It's pretty late. I'll
grab my gear and head to the barn, I'll
see you tomorrow." She touched his arm, then
dropped her hand; they faced each other, when
he abruptly said "I need to go." She
took a step back, looked down; tears filled her eyes;
she knew he had to leave; but when she cries,

Josiah wanted to kiss her tears, but
closed the door behind himself, asking, *What
am I to do?* Knowing that he valued
Job; respected him; and never viewed
injuring Job; if so, he'd be screwed.

Stanza 52

*J*ob was helped from the small wagon; as he
looked up to see Josiah walking in
his direction. "Commander," Job breathed in.
"Do not embrace me, for the pain is too
great when I'm touched." "I am sorry that you
are in this horrific condition, be
it an illness from God, or contagious.
I'm sure this sickness has made you anxious
especially to this point. Somewhere, Sir,
there is a cause. I know that if I were
you … no, I just can't imagine that He
would bring this disease on a priest. Your friends
are wrong to say that you hide sin—depends
on much more then supposition. I judge
you not." "Some friends, some family, misjudge
him," added Kallista, shaking her head; she
was filled with sorrow over this dread.
"He had a seriously bad time," said
his brother Eli. They all assisted
Job into the house—Eli persisted
in giving graphic details—nonstop
"The overnight camping was…" Kallista

cut him off. "I understand Eli." A
nervous Kallista physically sensed
the acute silence and her hands tensed;
she shook them like wringing wet hands to stop
the tingling. After Job was on his bed,
Eli said goodbye. Job sat for awhile; said,
"Josiah we can talk later in the
day." They nodded, Josiah thought that *the
day was going to be long*. He walked
to the kitchen; she went to him; he balked;
she cried on his shoulder; then they talked.

Stanza 53

"Throughout the early months, I often prayed
to dead children and my father—to no
avail. Job, more and more had grown worse; no
affection nor comfort to me, and
that grew worse as well. Almost two years, and
I'm still young; I realize that I've paid
a price most mothers and wives will never
comprehend; Job, doubtless will die; however,
I'm finding some peace, but not as a wife."
"I can't say that I understand, but life
can be a bitch, especially in your
case: young, beautiful, sensitive, and...well,
I'm getting off track. Forgive me. I'd tell
you other things, if you were not married;
although natural beauty is varied,
your Greek beauty is what a man looks for.
I am done talking," said Josiah looking

deep into her eyes. "I must start cooking
for Job; he'll be up soon," Kallista said.
"After he eats something, if he leaves bed,
he wanted to talk to you," she added.
Josiah caught the scent of her perfume;
rolled his eyes; sighed softly; left the room.
Job awakened, but could not leave the bed
so she took him what he wanted: she said,
"Here's the broth Job." She sat; he was padded
by blankets and pillows. "Did Josiah
leave for home?" he questioned. "Oh my, I ah
hope not." "No he is out back near the well,"
Kallista pointed with the spoon. "Please tell
him to come in, for I've finished eating."
Josiah, feeling a bit awkward; their meeting
still went well—not without some comforting.

Stanza 54

"Josiah, I've been worried more about
Kallista than my ailments. Words, and
sentences are stiff, monotone; by damn,
she mopes around like a hurt kitten or
a wounded calf. I think it's too much for
her, I mean that I am too much. The doubt
is great and burdens her." Josiah asked,
"What doubt do you speak of?" "She masked
her religion, and is not sure of God's
plan for our lives. Then she questions and prods

me for answers I don't know. I thought of
divorce for her sake; I will soon die. Love
is all but gone. Days of anger, I shove
the kitchen table, and it frightens her;
and the things she screams at me reflects pure
hatred for my condition, and our love.
I believe that my love is simply not
enough now. Her pointed words, *God forgot
about me* ring in my ears at night. We
are a lost pair." Job wept with pain. "Is she
getting better?" said Josiah trying
to harmonize what Job had said today
and with what he had witnessed yesterday
with Kallista. Job became quite tired;
asked Josiah to lay him back; mired
thoughts, sharp pain, and open sores throbbing,
he moaned as he was helped. He never
answered Josiah, for this endeavor
caused him to fall fast asleep. Josiah
slipped to the kitchen. "A pariah
is a better friend. I couldn't comfort him;
his face looked tired; eyes red, and dim;
Job's recovering, I fear, less than slim.

Stanza 55

"I hope like hell that he is not leaving.
The *Skin to Skin Campaign* would fail
and that would piss me off. He'll not derail
me, nor my extensive plans. Job believes

that he will die, so do I. If he leaves
this world, I win a big *if*, meaning,
of course, Light loses. Josiah must stay
and somehow be tempted to make her stray
or make love to him. Let's get rid of his
guiltiness by being taken in, his
own words, by her *pure loveliness*. Look he
is heading to get his stallion, and she
is following him to the barn—Yes! See,
she through her arms around him. Shit I thought
we had lost the battle. Josiah brought
us the victory. If Job could surmise, we
could do the rest in his brain. Mortals are
good at over thinking; strain good sense; mar
their lives. The barn incident is complete;
they will talk; rationalize what happened, beat
themselves with a smidgen of guilt; and
go bed. Phew, what a night in Uz. Damn
I'm good. Nothing too complex. Fallen man
is almost predictable: blames me, Light,
fate, or others for his shortcomings. Might
as well discard the dreadful rules—and
start over." Dark was always happy when
an unavailable woman—virgin
or married, sinned to please a man;
complexity—intensifies scheme; man
thrills Dark and his demons. "It's damnation
that frightens humans; miscalculation
worries spirits; but that is Light's creation."

CANTO ELEVEN

Stanza 56

Josiah left rather suddenly, but
had vowed to Kallista to return.
Job said, "You seem happier, an upturn
in spirits. I'm glad." She smiled the way
she had in the past. "I've had a good day,"
she said lifting a candle; warmed by what
she had done with Job's friend before riding
away. She must be cautious, providing
his care without causing one suspicion,
for she did not want to cause dejection
in Job's critical health nor his psyche.
They sat silent across from each other
at their table sipping wine. Another
long evening staring at goblets, or
hearing Job utter sporadic groans, or
asking to do something for him, for she
did not care tonight. She thought about a
future; lighted other oil lamps; a
cough, then Job said, "I've cited Light's law as
to why mankind must accept trouble as
well as blessing. The oath I've taken, I
will keep to my death. Most speak foolishness."
"Job, I will tell you just what foolishness…"
she held her mouth. "I'm sorry. I don't wish
to upset you just because of anguish."
"Not to worry. You've been having what I

call a superior day." She was pleased;
remembered a vision she had received:
Persephone came by way of the sky;
she lighted the heavens; opened my
mind with a bright streak of light; awaken,
she did on my bed, I was not mistaken;
she told me not to fear not be shaken.

Stanza 57

"Are you going to help me to bed?" Job had
asked snapping her out of her thoughts. "Yes, I
am," she said pushing her chair back. "That sigh
sounded as though pain is present." He said
nothing. He did appreciate that dread
had abated. "Wow, Tatterius, had
the insight to trick Kallista. That was
a stroke of genius; I'm glad that was
my idea. The Greek god's angle I
call it. Gods will appear, intensify
my second minor champagne: *Shame and Blame.*
This extensive variety of Greek
major and minor deities, so I'll
seek prime purposes that I require;
Thanatos is next to speak and inspire
Kallista; how gullible too; her claim
that *Job made me do it* will soon prove false,
when tender hearted women meets, who else,
the tender hearted deity—god of
non-violent death visits her. A love
touch by him, and then death. Great idea.

My god, not even I'm allowed to do
that." "Master, when do I begin to screw
things up?" asked Tatterius. "Tonight,"
Dark began, "but enter before daylight."
Kallista found sleep; then, *could it be a
vision* she thought; suddenly Thanatos
appeared in a vision: "Fear not," a loss
of words struck her tongue; quieted her;
"I am only hear to gently assure
you of peace. Mortals need rest and can find
it with me. I will blot out pain in kind
fashion, and you will leave them all behind."

Stanza 58

Kallista heard him speak in perfect Greek;
she sensed all miseries lifting from
her very being. The relief had come
 as a warm flowing movement from within.
"I will revisit in three nights; and in
the same form. Khaîre." "Goodbye," in a weak
voice, she said in return. Dark walloped
Tatterius' shoulder. "Developed
your own strategy? What the hell is this
three days? Josiah is returning; is
planning to take her away; and you give
her three days." "When will he arrive?" asked
Airlie."FYI mister , I'm aghast
and most importantly at his blunder,"
Dark said pointing to the blunder wonder.

"I'll be perplexed as long as I live;
why can't get our act together with
Kallista and Job. Wait a minute," with
his hand in the air; his head tilted, he
grinned, "Josiah stopped for the night; he
made a re-acquaintance with a former
lover. He won't arrive for three and a
half days—his stallion has gone lame, what a
shame. Tatterius—you're saved, or should I
say Thanatos." Dark was much better. I
hope that the shoulder I whacked through armor,
is better," he said giving him a one
arm hug. You will succeed in the long run."
Everyone seemed jovial in Dark's
lair. Airlie said, "Life is full of question marks."
Implicatus liked that, and laughed because
Airlie, without warning spits out a clause—
that is unrelated; Dark grins; withdraws.

Stanza 59

*D*ark sat tapping his nails on his throne. He
thought, *Will I win Shame and Blame? Will it bring
me a bigger prize like re-instatement? The string
attached to any chance of becoming Lucifer again
is changing my attitude a tad.* "Vain,
I suppose, to think of such a thing," he
mumbled. "What is it?" he barked; Airlie
approached. "Troops are ready for early
inspection." A hush soon permeated

Dark's lush palace. Demons, all created
for service; aligned to obey Dark at
his impulsive command, even before
the Fall. A thousand trained demons for war
stood at attention in each, straight column.
There was quiet breathing, all was solemn.
"Thank you. Quite nice. Dismissed," Dark said. At
that they broke up and scurried to duties.
"Tatterius, there will be penalties
if you screw up again. Go to Uz and
check on the lovely couple, sick Job and
attractive Kallista. Make sure that she
dwells on the escaping with the handsome
Josiah. Report to me of gladsome
expressions or statements from Kallista.
Prime her for the decision to leave, a
slip up could cost us a defeat, for she
alone can spoil the Shame and Blame Campaign.
This effort is critical to retain
my slim hope of… never mind." *I'm possessed
or I'm gradually becoming possessed
by this design of being Lucifer
again,* he thought. Such a future loser—
no doubt; he felt held by the jugular.

Stanza 60

For Job, long nights lingered into a day;
this one was chilly and breezy as he
sorted three shards of broken pottery
for scraping constantly itching skin to

find relief; a daily chore; each day to do;
and a left eye irritation today;
leaking gray and red fluid from a sore
on his forehead; was futile anymore
to attempt herbal paste for it dried,
cracked, and seeped. Kallista had cried
when she had to care for his infected
spots; he thought these ugly spots effected
their bond, and caused him to feel dejected.
Hairline wounds appeared, and now his sight was
being damaged. Strong man to weak man was
his quiet mantra. He had suspected
that the blackening on his skin had been
the cause of bruising. What dreadful chagrin
to even ask Kallista a question
concerning his horrific condition.
"My wife, how are you today? I hope that
your mood is yet improved. Kallista,
what's wrong?" She had been startled. Josiah
was on her mind as she stared at the barn.
"Oh, I was just thinking about the darn
animals we have in our yard, and that
they'll all survive I'm sure," she lied.
Kallista could hardly wait or abide
by her promise not to tell Job about
leaving him. She just wanted to get out.
Josiah, she now believed possessed
her; couldn't stand another day stressed;
for in his arms, felt completely blessed.

Stanza 61

"I wonder why Josiah never said
goodbye," Job said. "You had been sleeping when
he left." Job had a puzzled look, and then
said, "Is he returning soon?" She felt a
bit uncomfortable, and lately a
great amount of love, and cautiously said,
"I believe that he will be here in a
another day." "All right, if Josiah
said that, he'll be here," Job concluded.
She was glad that Job hadn't alluded
to anything else. She was afraid of
giving away her plan, and never thought
about hurting him, but there was no thought
about turning back either. One of three
leathery patches began to itch; he
needed warmed beeswax to soothe the itch. Love,
at least, old love made Kallista get the
beeswax; warm it for spots on his back; a
promise made six months ago, pressed
her to do this for him. Her time progressed
slowly the last two days, but doing this
for Job had eased her conscience, for pressing
on her mind: Josiah; fingers messing
with his hair; undressing him; and making love.
Nothing was left; nothing needed above
him. This would be a grand new life; and this
was good for her; forgetting unpleasant
events; like death, her father; at present—

all of her future looked bright as she had
been told by Thanatos not be sad.
She helped Job get into bed, maybe,
the last time; his brother would have to be
the one to help; Job would have to agree.

Stanza 62

Two nights passed; Job was in bed fast asleep.
Kallista dosed off, but was abruptly
awakened by Thanatos. "Fear not. Be
not concerned. This is the third night; I had
promised to materialize to you. Be glad,
tonight you may choose everlasting sleep,
or have me blot out injuries, heartache,
and disorder—all three, just for your sake,
if you wish. Touch my thigh, and in three days,
you will find solace." "This news deserves praise,
but, will I have Josiah?" "He will be
here at noon; by the fifth hour you will
flee; have your wish. Farewell. "Now my goodwill
could reward me." she looked about but could
not see him; he had vanished. "I should
congratulate you Tatterius; see,
until that crucial hour, I'll wait,"
said Dark. Sunrise brought soft light to abate
the night. Kallista hugged herself, and
smiled as she rolled from side to side, and
thought of Josiah. "Kallista, are you
awake?" asked Job. "I'll be right there."

She had a wonderful feeling; nowhere
would she rather be than with Josiah;
where would they live? She thought, would they have a
child? One thought after another; she knew
that they were right for each other, she could
hardly wait for noon to arrive; he would
sweep her up in his arms, and steal her
away. "I am coming Job. I have pure
date honey syrup, olive oil, and
bread." She scurried around; felt young again;
Josiah had money, was handsome; all was grand.

Stanza 63

Noon arrived, and Kallista heard a
horse neighing and snorting as her heart skipped
a beat; she couldn't move. Job looked, then quipped,
"That Josiah is true to his word; here
he is. Go let him in. I did not hear
the horse until it was near the house. A
man like him is probably hungry.
There is plenty of food." Job felt angry,
 for the excitement had made him cough and
wheeze. He got up to go lie down again,
when the door opened. "Here, here Job, let me
help," Josiah said grabbing his arm. He
added, "I saw your brother Eli. He
said that he would see you in a few days.
Here now lie down; let me prop you up. Days
are getting worse for you I guess. I see

that you seem weaker. Try to rest my friend."
He watched Job fall asleep, and then when
he could, slipped quietly to the room
where Kallista had been waiting. "There's gloom
in this kitchen," he teased her. "Don't do that,"
she said throwing her arms around him. He
at once responded. Their passion might be
something they needed to go to the barn
to complete—they did. Moving from the barn,
he was looking down at the ground; she at
him. "What is it?" she questioned. "Oh, nothing.
"You seem like there is something is bothering
you." Josiah smiled at her. "Let me
grab a few items, and we can leave." He
said, "All right, but let's sit outside awhile
over there by the rock." He loved her smile
as they sat. "You would not like my lifestyle."

Stanza 64

"Let me tell you about daily life. I
am a women, full of vigor, passion,
and life." Her face was flush; her affection
for him began to make him uneasy;
doubt crossed his mind; was strangely queasy,
like oppression. "What is wrong with you? I
sense it." "We have been acquainted," he said,
"for many years, and yet, when you had wed
I had still thought repeatedly, *my god
how beautiful she is*, and I was awed

at your fresh beauty from the first time I had
met you at sixteen. Now a beautiful
twenty-nine year old; undisputable
compared to any women. Ten days
ago, I had made love to her in ways
I could not explain. Your tenderness had
been something I had dreamed about in
the past. You had possessed me; toxin
to my mind; what I am saying is that
I have loved you for a long time. At
that, she said, "Josiah, what then is the
problem?" After a short pause, he said, "Job;
I am sorry, I didn't want to probe."
"There is no query, he will die soon, then
I'm given to his older brother, when
all is settled, like chattel or goods. The
further truth is, frankly, as said one day—
*How am I expected to feel the way
we're treated with—sickness and death. Instruct
this Greek mind. Curse your God and die. We're fucked.*
Then I left the room, and things have turned worse.
We stopped sleeping together a nurse
is what I had become; life at its worst."

Stanza 65

When the two entered the house, Job was at
the table. "I had eaten a piece of
bread. Anyway, it's good to see both of
you." Josiah said, "Did you have a good
nap?" "Indeed I did. Those wheezing spells would

usually come on me at night. That
is something that comes with whatever I
have. I feel weaker today, and my
left eye has a burning sensation." He
looked up at Josiah, head back; he
tilted it to the left side, squinted his
left eye at him. "What a grand gesture
for you to come." "Job, it is my pleasure."
"Would you two men like a bite to eat?" asked
Kallista trying to be herself, masked
every word and action, because this
was her last day in Uz. "Josiah, been
in any wars lately?" "I suppose ten
weeks ago near Jericho. I was actually
just an advisor; contractually
consult; only killed eight men this last time."
"I miss the comradeship of fighting men;
the sting of battle; the faithful omen
when Light leads us; and the exaltation
of victory. I like expectation
of archangels aiding warriors. Onetime…"
Job had a short coughing jag from talking.
Josiah decided to go walking
and headed for the barn. Kallista was
busy cleaning up. She saw that it was
nearly the sixth hour. Two more to go.
She tapped her foot; asked Job to show
any new boils; her face was aglow.

Stanza 66

Job decided to nap; tired; the afternoon exertion and seeing Josiah
had been too much for his condition—a
worsening malady. Kallista knew
that in less than two hours, she had to
help Job into bed; get her things; after,
she had to send a message to Eli
through a slave that he must come soon, and why.
Suddenly she heard a horse at a full
gallop—it was Josiah startling the bull
who scampered away. *Where was he going?*
she thought as her slave came in unknowing
what was meant by all of this; happening
too quickly. Kallista had a message
from Josiah: *I must leave.* This presage
was the foreshadow she had feared. "Going
without me," Kallista cried out as she
ran to the barn; grabbed Job's stallion; she
was leaving it all behind; and swiftly
went after Josiah. Here' s exactly
why she hadn't trusted him. She could see
him in the distance. She pressed the horse to
go faster. She was gaining on him; too
far to go back; it was an hour out when
Josiah, with a premonition, then
turned to see her. She lifted quickly
on her horse and waved. As she did, her
horse tumbled forward and fell, throwing her
in the air—she broke her neck on the fall.

Josiah galloped toward her; all
he thought about—Kallista— too late. He
jumped down from his horse; lifted her gently
in his arms. Held her; kissed her; it was four-fifty.

Stanza 67

*J*ob and Eli were in the house when news
arrived about Kallista's tragic
death. As Josiah carried her, the fabric
on her clothes caught the door handle; he said,
"She had been bringing me food." Eli said
"You had left in a hurry, giving a ruse
to a slave that you must leave." "That was no
sham. I had to leave because of pact, oh,
what's your point Eli? Wait, let me lay her
on her bed." He wiped his eyes. "Joffa, per
contract, this time," he continued.
Job went in to sit by his wife. Rent his clothes;
wailed; punched the bed; kissed her cheek; knows
nothing of her affair. The husband priest
wept; family all dead; he said, "Al least
perhaps, she has found peace." Discontinued
talking, for he could not stop lamenting.
Eli said, "What was she doing riding
out that far?" "She was bringing food, you see,
for my journey to Joffa." "Oh, makes me
fully understand." "If Job does not mind,
I will leave in the morning." "Probably
a good idea before ungodly
and speculative inquiries start.

People are ruthless; they cut through the heart."
"I know that Job will mourn for some time; kind
relatives and friends will assist in the
ritual. "She will be buried in the
cave of Job north of Uz with his children.
Our brothers, sisters-in-law, and brethren
will provide the things he needs," said Eli.
Josiah left for the barn to sleep; *why
did this happen* he thought; he's the bad guy.

CANTO TWELVE

Stanza 68

"Oh my god, Tatterius. You got things
done by ten to five. That accident, or
was it, had certainly helped you, and more
of these needed victories are what I,
I mean, that we want. Skin to Skin—my, my,
that was good. Lust is a fabulous thing,
one of my favorite tools. Shame and Blame
Campaign—stupendous—guilt, disgrace, and lame
attempts to cover-up lies. Beguiling
works so often when twisting truth," smiling
Dark said." I should use it more. These were two
enormous winning campaigns. Wow! I am too
happy. What does Light think about the two
battles he had just lost? Nevertheless,
that's brilliant that you had left such a mess
in Uz. Strictly from my unrighteous view,
Job is our target—no Greek or foreign
gods with this priest, like the misfits, herein
known as—adulterous and widower.
Phew, I'm proud of myself—a follower—
not! Although, I might, if Light would review
history before man came along. Well,
spilled milk and all that. We're back to the hell
on earth. We need a new campaign. Something
catchy to get our brains around. Nothing
will stop me from winning Light's end review

of me for defeating Job. "What is the
final review?" asked Airlie. "It's a
review at the end of things." "Oh, I see."
That was quite easy Dark thought. "I will be
in Uz tomorrow to craft more debris.
Job is mourning; women cleansing body;
can't foresee more havoc; can't impede me."

Stanza 69

A week passed; Light came to Job and said,
"You have completed the lengthy trial
of persecution on you for awhile
that found you innocent of cursing me,
except for the time you questioned me;
queried me; be mute as one who's dead.
Brace yourself you man," said Light out of a
furious storm. "I'm omnipotent; the
trustworthy God; omnipresent showing
mercy in love; a creator of things
good; a protector of the weak; and a
supporter of the strong." "I know that you
are the true God," said Job. "I told you to
be still." Light looked at Eliphaz, "I am
angry at you and your friends; you exam
Job, by misrepresenting me. Make a
sacrifice of seven bulls, seven
rams, but take them to Job so that heaven
will see your sacrifice. Job will pray for
you, and his interceding prayer for
each of you, I do accept, so that your

punishment is not brought against you for
your foolishness—Job did do right. Abhor
what is right again or punishment will
follow. None of you said anything ill
or derogatory against me. For
Job, who had been a wealthy man, shall have
twice as much. Job, for seven months you have
gone from small discomfort to sheer anguish;
therefore, in just three weeks I shall vanquish
this enemy of torment, beginning
today. You have been faithful—not sinning;
there's something that I must be completing."

Stanza 70

Dark asked for an audience with Light.
"What is it Dark?" "I am in a bit of
a quandary," he said; he was out of
sorts; having a tough time untwisting his
usually quick witted tongue. "This is
it; I clearly won two of my scraps, Light;
decisive victories that should mean a little:
Campaigns *Skin to Skin* and *Shame and Blame*." "It'll
be quite difficult for me, but I had
permitted you to have these very sad,
distressing victories." "What! Maddening!
This is unjust; unmitigated gall;
I thought that I had a chance to win all:
my name back; my status; a forgiven
soul." Light said, "Lucifer had been given
that name *bright morning star*, how saddening,

that an honest nature and brilliance,
inventive of things good, resilience,
and yet, with supreme qualities, had not
contemplated the consequences. Caught
in pride as commander of half of my
angels; you turned against me with the
very will I had given to you; the
audacity to have convinced one-
third of all angels to desert me; done
with narcissistic pride; commanded my
archangels, led by Michael, to have you
thrown from this celestial palace—crew
and all; left items necessary for
upcoming work; then striped power; swore:
that you could not bring death to humans, at
the time of their creation, Thereat,
you cannot have that superb name—that's that."

Stanza 71

Light went further. "As for your soul, it is
dark as crimson." Dark softened his voice, "You
had been compassionate not to subdue,
my will. What must I do to find your grace?"
Dark waited, then suddenly Light said, "Grace?
Dark's eyes squeezed out hot, red tears; but his
body remained at-ease. Light told him
that he had been cursed—life would be grim.
Light could see that Dark's temperament was
growing unstable. "Man, as loving as
I could make them, had been formed lower

than angels. You had privileges humans
could not imagine. I gave all humans
a will, but it failed—love demands will.
I had thought that you and I had a still
more wonderful bond; you are a sower
of deception, but... never mind. Go back
to roaming the earth." Dark—thought of a crack.
"A-tten-tion. Dismissed." Dark grumbled as he
did an about-face, and marched straight to flee
through the Celestial opening, and
fell toward the earth faster than lightning.
Lucifer had been handsome—now a thing;
a fiend, almost unimaginable;
could change his countenance compatible
with his need; could look like anyone; and
able to take on the appearance of
anything. Light was correct to think of
the old relationship, but not renew
the bond with such a beast. At least, he knew
that at this time it would be a tragic
error to attempt any catholic
or partial absolution—too drastic.

Stanza 72

Dark cracked the air in his palace with
a blast, "What the hell. We won two of the
three battles; did what we were to do." A
roar from demons sounded in support,
not fully understanding Dark's report.
"We caused Job's torment and trials; with

dispatch we killed his children, and in the
end, killed his wife. We all but razed the
Land of Uz; stirred up the Sabeans and
had Job and his army, kill wave and band
after band of them, and what do we get—
an audience with Light. He reminded
me of the past, then sent me blindsided
directly back to here. This is shit; I
cannot say it any plainer, but I
may have another chance when Job is bet
against again." Tatterius asked,
"What did Light say?" Dark said, "He is aghast
when he learns of the affair of the pair:
Josiah and Kallista—pretty fair
wife; he will have been restored—with strength
that is double. Knowing him, he will most
definitely attempt revenge and post
an award on Josiah to avenge
his wife's honor—if she had had a tinge.
Job will find justice; go to any length
for the Law of Light—to the guilty—death.
An adulterer should not live—the breath
that Light had given shall be snuffed out.
Have no misgivings, Job will go about
trying to remain devout and holy;
searching to fight against all unholy
men; and to do it in haste not slowly."

Stanza 73

"Light knows things before the final result—
within the law of the will. Shortly a
Priest, in three weeks will initiate the
assault on his enemy, Josiah,
with justifiable anger; with a
sword of righteousness; first, he must consult
Light. He is packing provisions for his
journey; his military gear; riches—
torn pages of God's Law. Let's watch as it
develops." Dark and three of his imps flit
into the nearest oak tree to Job's house
three and a half weeks after he had been
completely healed. "Look. His condition
is unbelievable," said Airlie. "That
is great, just watch," said Dark. "Phew, that
is amazing swordsmanship. The louse,
Josiah doesn't stand a chance—did you
see the oak table split in half?" *I too
wondered about that* thought Airlie, and *why
had Dark continued to talk*. "Heard that. My
you forget so often—be careful what
you think around me. Let's come back later,"
Dark said. "Tired of this imitator."
Job dosed off with a quote from pre-Torah:
"Noah, a righteous man, blameless, a
good man among people of his time…" What
a great morning he thought; he was soon drawn
to birds chirping and the soft noise of dawn.
The silence in the house, made his senses

notice a scent, quickly his defenses
rose up like old sores. On a dresser was
an open bottle of oil used as
protection for hair—out of ideas.

Stanza 74

Kallista was still there. He was out of
options concerning her, after Eli
had shared some of his thoughts about her lie
about Josiah. Job realized that
her self-centered love had been based on flat-
out self-preservation that could parch love
like a wilted rose. He gathered up all
of her belongings and burned them. The gall
she had possessed; the shallow thinking;
but how beautiful, although unthinking.
He traded his stallion for a younger,
yet well trained steed, fit to fight against
any rival, no matter how immense.
A warrior, especially a chief
among men, needs such a horse; relief
in mind is vital to put asunder
the enemy. Concentration of horse
and rider—Job required. Of course,
there was much more: gathering an army;
locating Josiah; and hopefully
some preparation for the advancement
of other treacherous endeavors meant
to destroy him. Thus he had to augment
his forces. He thought that Light had doubled

his strength for a reason, and this had troubled
him; he felt that nothing would circumvent
him; he had known as a past commander:
he ought to be prepared, free of slander
and misgiving; this meant that he had to
be exceedingly organized too.
Two thousand fighting men came under his
command; regretted that it came to this;
knew well that he had done nothing amiss.

Stanza 75

Tatterius enters the great torch lit
hall, behind—Implicatus and Airlie
all in perfect cadence and step; the three
halt before Dark' gold thrown; execute
a left-face; snap to attention; salute;
then tensely wait for a response to it.
Their commander returns a crisp greeting,
"At-ease. I summoned you to this meeting
because this warrior-priest is marching
to the Great Sea. Japho, where he's planning
to find and fight Josiah—hand to hand,
is not quite as I, nor he, had figured.
A surprise is waiting, configured
to bring down a hundred men at once.
Job had caught a glimpse of it; pounced
on two ships, obliterating all; every hand
went into the sea, and were never found.
This Lotan is a monster that will drowned
anyone within one hundred feet. It

is a seven-headed beast—get this—it
is a serpent. How apropos. Crafted
by me, of course, and I had not drafted
any help. This grand monster has lasted
more than five hundred thousand years. I had
wanted him created—wow I am glad
to have that ability—not shafted
entirely." Dark dismissed his minions
with strict orders to tempt the sad millions
of humans, especially, the priest, Job
the most prominent target on the globe.
Job marched his army to Japho; made
camp near the city. His men were afraid
of Josiah—but true to the crusade.

Stanza 76

A slumbering mammoth crocodile
arose out of the Merrimack River
wetlands; an awful nightmare; a giver
of painful death; it mangled anyone
who came close; eaten not for food—for fun;
men from the village did their best, while
many tossed in the air, caught in its mouth;
hiccup, then he swallowed. A large loudmouth,
a broad man, came to save—quickly eaten.
No one or anything could have beaten
that enormous monster. It was devouring
screaming people; then cries of help reached
Job. He strapped on his scabbard; breached
the gap between the monster and victims;

ran swiftly to aid locals; poor pilgrims
who had just now heard of the beast; then cowering;
waddled and ambled to a halt—then Job saw
monster. He drew his sword; without flaw,
cut air with sword; noticed—beast's right front foot
was bleeding; it must have been an offshoot
from a injury in the river. It
swung its huge tail at him; but he
jumped over it. The beast in a frenzy
now focused on Job. Without much thought
the warrior ran speedily, as taught,
in the opposite direction; looked it
in the eyes as it ambled; found a chance;
jumped to its head; then firmed his stance;
but it began to brace its tail, so
that it could roll over to crush its foe.
Job leaped to a large tree; to the ground;
as the monster began to move, to bound
to its feet; Job—unlike any man found.

Stanza 77

Job sprung to the top of the beast, with sword
in both hands; thrusting it as it came straight
down into the head and brain—its vast weight
slumped in death like a small tremor. "Shut
up! This is not right," said Dark. "My god, what
just happened? Is this really Light's word?
This is a bit over the top." Job slid
down the tail after wiping sword amid
the scales; looked up to see a crowd

forming; they were singing praises so loud
that Job couldn't understand. The mayor
of the city asked him, "Who are you sir?
Only a god could have killed him; and were
it not for you, many more would be dead.
Come into our city to dine," he said.
"Very well. First allow me confer
with my commanders, and choose three men to
accompany me." The pair agreed to
meet later. Job said to his three leaders
that he was going to ask town leaders
questions as to the place of where the cur
Josiah was last seen. The men had a
surprise gift for him: a bloody claw, a
cleaned up bloody claw from the beast. He
smiled, placed the claw in his tent. He
left strict orders: "We all must watch; concur
with me that Josiah will fight only
me. Tell him. Report immediately
to me, any contact with him. I will
come quickly to face him, and I will grill
him for the truth. Job attended the town
event; mayor celebrated around
the city; Job—talk of the entire town.

Stanza 78

Job explained to his men that no one
should eat the flesh of the monster for it
is forbidden food that would not befit
the human body for consumption, for

it could cause serious illness. "Abhor
it, as our Lord had instructed. The One
we must rely on," Job explained. The
mayor agreed with Job; could not stop the
people. The beast's blood had a foul
odor; the armor like hide was foul
with parasites; merchants insisted that
they were planning to craft sandals for the
poor. Job had become agitated; the
entire matter was keeping him in
the city too long. Besides, he in
all sincerity and humbleness, felt that
at that time it was a local issue.
The feast was joyous, despite some issues,
for the people found a sense of peace as
well. Job told them, "Keep in mind: our God has
allowed me to slay it, even though He
had created it." "Why would our God make
such a monstrous animal that could rake
in people like a child picks up small
toys, then kills and scares hundreds, can't recall
a scene like this—ever?" the deputy
mayor asked. Job said, "Light is creator
of all life, and at that time, its nature
had a specific purpose: to show the
Creator's power and majesty; the
other reason had been to warn humans
of His judgment against all evil clans;
even personal sin—look to His plans."

Stanza 79

"There is another reason: perhaps the
old beast was dying." Numerous people
pressed and bumped against him; a temple
of a pagan god with a calf relief
loomed above; shook his head in disbelief;
as he tried to leave the city; a
multitude followed him with queries;
never before had he inquiries
at that pace; he smiled, nodded, as his
men pulled him through the throng, while this
merrymaking continued, if fact,
it went on through the whole night. The mayor,
city council, merchants and many more
patted his back, gave medals, pieces of
gold and silver, and offered an above
average sum to stave-off an attack
of another beast or foreign army.
He explained that he and his army
were on a mission. He talked privately
with the devout mayor, but concisely.
Job left Japho with a reward of a
glossy, seven ounce medal—pure gold; and
that Josiah had gone to give a hand
in Kittim to assist in the fierce fight
against Greeks attacking them after light
of day. The fighting has been brutal, a
bloodbath, some say. The attacks have come
from the north. Job secured large ships from
seven merchants, and three from the city

had been given for his journey. Many
ships and boats had been badly damaged by
a severe storm—no one sought to deny
him; in fact, it was hard to say goodbye.

Stanza 80

The entire city had feared that
another behemouth would be lurking
in the sea, and wanted Job's supporting
their efforts to defeat it; with his sword.
"I must aid Kittim; I cannot ignore
their dire need; my vast army is at
once ready to offer my trained force.
My reinforcements could alter the course
or outcome," Job explained. The city
wished them well. Job felt a bit guilty
knowing that his primary goal was to
find Josiah—to kill him. He would not
do a thing to Josiah, if Light thought
that Josiah had been falsely accused.
Job never did anything when confused
or when a gut feeling told him not to
proceed. Almost four hours had passed
before they had loaded the ten ships vast
cargo bays with troops, gear, five horses, and
provisions. Men and horses had to stand
the majority of the twelve hour
ordeal—sailing the Great Sea. Job sat
in silence, in the bow, and peering at
the shore line, miles away; thinking of

Kallista, the fifteen year girl of
Kittim who he had loved; the grand dower
he had received upon wedding her; her
kind parents and siblings; in dismay, blur
fogged his mind as he remembered her
lifeless form. Joseph, his top commander
called out, "Sir, we will approach Kittim
in three hours. The fighting will be grim,
but I have faith in you, and Elohim."

Stanza 81

"It will take us, at least, three hours to
disembark with all equipment, and
form our columns." "That sounds about right, and
keep in mind that I had heard of the fierce
fighting. In order to properly pierce
defenses, I need the commanders to
meet me for a briefing as soon as we
disembark." "Yes sir," said Joseph, as he
turned and went to inform the leaders.
"We may have to commandeer three cedars
from seven of the ships to complete the
shelter for the officers." "Very well."
said Job, "I will explain this to dispel
any concerns and tell each captain
that all boards will be replaced." "I happen
to know personally" said Joseph, " the
captains are not concerned, for you had
saved their city." "Keep an account, add
it correctly, and make sure I get that

list," said Job. He looked at the Great Sea; sat
down; and then, saw in the distance, along
the horizon, Kittim. This brought very strong
feelings, but he didn't wish to do wrong:
Josiah will get his just reward. Waves
began to lift the bow; he thought of graves,
the eternal watery graves below. *Belonging to a great mission of hope was more important than life,* he thought. Raging war
was less than an hour away. Soon they
landed, and began to unload to enter the fray
It had taken them three hours, for twelve
thousand fresh warriors, supplies to delve
into this fight—Job now, must find resolve.

Stanza 82

Under Job's command they marched north of
Kittim to join the forces of their allies.
Troops divided into two flanks; valley's
western edge had a road winding down to
the shallow bottom; the other flank, to
 the eastern side along the slopping of
rolling edge to the basin; but Job had
formulated a plan: two flanks, and add
three thousand of the best for a frontal
assault, backing up Kittim's jumbled,
but faithful forces that were straight ahead
of him; he could see the fighting, assessed
it. "Men, Light will fight with us, but our best

is expected. Let us push right through the
middle; follow me." With shouts and screams, the
companies headed down the slope; the dead
were everywhere; clanging of swords; arrows
flying through the air; as distance narrows
between the armies, spears went their wished-for
routes, one finding Josiah. Job went for
the spear thrower that had killed him; then
went to tend to Josiah, who had slain
more than a thousand that week. He in pain,
and weak, looked in Job's eyes through tears. "I'm…"
He fell limp in Job's arms. Job whispered, "I'm
not a judge, my battlefield friend." Then
Job killed more than three hundred enemies;
at the end of day—one thousand. Treaties
began to be discussed among the Greek
generals; they knew the future was bleak
as to finding a victory. Job had
been unknown to them yesterday, for had
they known, nothing would had been ironclad.

Stanza 83

Warring Greeks came to an unsettling
agreement to remove themselves, and to
allow native non-combatant Greeks to
remain, for Hebrews and native Greeks had
lived together as ship builders; clad
in the same garments, sailors wrestling
with the Great Sea—almost three hundred years.
Nevertheless, the treaty was signed. Cheers

of joy spread amongst the troops, but now the
dead must be buried; ships repaired with the
cedar logs and planks Job had promised to
give; only seven men died—one had been
Josiah. Job was unsure; and chagrin
filled his soul because he wanted to see
Chara, his former mother-in-law; he
didn't know if she was living; needed to
ask around. He went through the marketplace
inquiring about her. The last place
he had looked, a man came up to him
and introduced himself. "I am Ibrim,
and I hear you are looking for Chara."
"Yes. She is my former Mother-in-law.
My wife, her daughter, had died by a flaw
in the horse's lower leg, a riding
mishap. I have been here fighting, guiding…"
"I understand why you are here, I saw
the battles, and I am grateful for what
you had done for our city, Kittim, but
I hope the treaty works," said Ibrim. "Ah,
anyway, Chara resides on Astra
in a fine house. Her widowed niece lives with
her to help her with the house chores, a blythe
sole. Her beauty—enchanting—the zenith."

Stanza 84

"Go straight up this street; at the corner turn
right; go about three hundred feet, and on
the right is her house." "I will after dawn

tomorrow. I have a staff briefing to
attend tonight. Thank you Ibrim. How do
you know the family?" asked Job. "To yearn
for your family, as I had, full of
indecision, until Aton, above
everyone in Kittim assured me that
I could make it here. So, I had that
to keep me here. I had known her husband
for many years. I am Hebrew and Greek;
he was pure Greek, but a very unique
and wonderfully kind. Fine man." "I hope
to see you tomorrow," said Job. To cope
with Kallista's suspicious demise, and
then have to explain the circumstance was
trying his spirit. Had it been because
he had been so ill? He had to end the
over-thinking, and he went off to the
staff meeting. It lasted until midnight
The next morning he had given orders:
"Pull down the seven officer's quarters;
repair ships by replacing cedar beams
and planks; tomorrow, by noon, by all means,
I plan to set sail." He then headed right
to Astra Road. He arrived; a woman
came to the door. Tears filled her eyes; no man
had meant so much to her besides her late
husband; she could not speak; his heart rate
increased; she looked at the sky; back to the
ground. Job waited; he knew it was Chara.
He could tell nothing about Kallista.

Stanza 85

"Come in Job," she said hugging him. "You look
terrific; you look more muscular than
the last time, and that had to be the span
of fifteen years when you had married
Kallista." "Thank you Chara. I've tarried
much too long. You too look good. Her head shook
back and forth. She sat down with him at the
table; they ate dates, olive oil, a
drink, and bread. "Now that you have eaten, tell
me about my dear Kallista, to quell
my questions," she requested. "You know, ten
children, a wonderful expanse of land,
and I had quit soldiering, and began
priestly pursuits; the tragedy which you
have certainly heard of by this time through
our letters and our trading of goods when
we are able to ship them to Kittim,"
Job began. Chara's mind was fixed on him.
"I believe that you are referring to
her sudden death," Chara nodded. "Can you
understand my reluctance in sharing
this with you? Tears filled her eyes. "It was
a riding mishap." He waited because
of the emotional nature of his
information. He went on, "Chara is
this too difficult?" "Yes and no. Comparing
my problem with your hardship is not fair,
but what is hard for me to understand; her despair
over having ten children only to

have them all die that day, and then to
die in a riding accident, the dread."
"Let's sit in this other room." "I'm home," said
someone. "It's your niece, Ahuda," she said.

Stanza 86

"My dearly beloved niece, who lives with me,
she said to Job. "Come in here and meet
my handsome son-in-law, Job, whose small fleet
is from Japho." "Where is Japho?" asked
Ahuda. "It is a great distance past
Crete, a shipping seaport on the Great Sea,"
said Chara, "and that is near to where your
cousin Kallista had lived." "Sir, your
reputation is well known. I have just
returned from the market, where men discussed
much about you." Ahuda said, "Are you,
the commander of the liberating
troops, that came to help?" Deliberating
each phrase, Ahuda said. "Yes," Job answered.
"You killed a beast in Japho? You captured…"
"Enough Ahuda," said Chara. "She's too
young to understand such things, although she
had been widowed for less than two years, she
is only twenty years old. Her husband
had been a fisherman, a firebrand
with a temper; sorry Ahuda; the
truth is the truth. He lost his life, and so
did the entire crew; it was a blow
to the city." "I am sorry to hear

An Epic of Job, The Biblical Warrior-Priest

that," said Job. Chara to him, "A seer
had advised Ahuda about the
death of her husband, and of the entire
crew, and that the future would not require,
goods for they would come to her, but she would
not have children with this sailor. She should
pray to find a kind man." Chara then told
Ahuda how Job had remained bold
but that there was much about him—untold.

Stanza 87

*J*ob returned to his commanders to
get a status report. The ships would be
ready late that day, but that only three
ships could be loaded with some equipment
before dark; the good news: the small shipment
of goods from Kittim would be on board too:
however, they were not able to set
sail until after dawn. The threat
of not signing the treaty finally
had passed, and all parties unkindly
went there ways. Job told his officers that
he was going to dinner. He sent word
by one of his assistants and spurred
him to Chara: he would accept her
invitation. He arrived after
purchasing some wine. He arrived at
just the right time to here Chara: "He lost
ten children and his wife, and at a great cost
to his health." "He looks very good today.

He also looks too young to have had a
brood of ten," said Ahuda. Chara said,
"I figured that he is turning forty."
"He makes my eyes feel good—he is hearty,"
said Ahuda. Job knocked at the door.
Ahuda briskly went to the door, for
she assumed it was Job. Ahuda said,
"Good afternoon." he nodded, "Good afternoon to you." "Welcome, Job, but hereafter
would you call me Huda?" They walked to the
kitchen; Job offered, "Ahuda is a
Hebrew name meaning *dearly loved*, and
by shortening it would alter the grand
meaning." She fanned her face with her hand.

Stanza 88

Chara told Job, "Ahuda's mother was
Hebrew, and having three sons, all with Greek
names, she insisted on the name to pique
the father's frustration. Ahuda kept
the name; had been teased—never inept;
her wit had made her the child that she was
and the beautiful woman that she is,
and that coincides with the meaning this
good name has meant to her mother and me."
"Chara you are so kind to say that," she
said looking at her aunt. "Whatever cause
Job has undertaken, his intention
has been moral; excuse the intrusion
into our dinner time, but Job, I must

An Epic of Job, The Biblical Warrior-Priest

tell Ahuda who you are, and I trust… "
A knock; Chara went to the door; it was
an officer to give Job an update.
Job stepped outside. Chara, lead by Fate,
continued to speak with her eager niece
about Job. "Job is a militia genius;
a skillfully trained self-defense fighter;
has a god-given strength that's mightier
than any; to the weak--fortifier;
intelligent insight to solve problems;
a duty driven eagerness that hems
enemies in; he defies fear; writers
will record the mighty deeds of this man
of God; and his God, he calls Light, began
speaking to him as a youth." "How do you
know such things about him, and are they true?"
asked Ahuda. "During the fighting here
in Kittim, I went to the market. There,
three of his men said—'no one could compare.'"

Stanza 89

"My cousin Kallista was extremely
lucky," said Ahuda. "Any woman
would, with great happiness, take that he-man.
Or should I say that he could have any
woman. Job is coming in with many
bottles of wine" she said." "It seemingly
appears that three officers came, and brought
the wine." "Is dinner ready? My men thought
that a few bottles of wine would be nice.

"That wine had to be an expensive price,
at least this bottle," Ahuda pointed
to the red wine." "Do not worry about
that. This fine family deserves, no doubt
the best. Chara, has been good to me." "And
I'll do the same." Ahuda caught—eyes and
smile of Chara. A bit disjointed,
Job attempted to talk about the meal.
In the evening, in a surreal
state of mind, Ahuda went outside to
speak with Job who was alone thinking through
his plans to return to Uz. Looking at
the sunset on the bay. They spoke of the
weather, the war, widowhood, and Chara,
and then she said, "It is hard to live without
a spouse." Job didn't answer. "I mean there's doubt
concerning the future, no lover that
gives you attention, no companionship;
similar enjoyment." "Relationship
is broad when speaking of spouses as one.
When Kallista died, I felt I had run
out of time, but Light had promised me
that He would bless me: enemies would flee;
life once again would have festivity."

Stanza 90

"Will you tell me more about my mother's
Hebrew faith? I have more of my father's
Greek features, but much more of my brother's
temperament, and little upbringing

in Hebrew." "I will briefly share a thing
or two about religions, cultures,
and any specific questions," Job said.
They had spent a few hours eating bread,
drinking wine, and talking when Chara came
to join them. Out of the blue, said, "To tame
a Greek is tough to do." Job said, "Where did
that come from? Thank you for being candid."
He then told her that they had a splendid
evening talking, and what they had been
discussing. Chara reminded again
that Ahuda's beauty is from enchanted
 Greek heritage."They laughed, but Job had
noticed her youthfulness, liveliness; add
her beautifully sculptured face—body
and one could see, that she would embody
everything any man would want or need.
Job caught himself staring, and Ahuda
did too. "Well I had better get back. The
troops are expecting me; actually
they had expected me earlier, factually,
I should not have been here for dinner—creed:
all things happen for a reason. We leave
in the late morning, for we must achieve
our goals and time tables. What a grand
host you are Chara. I have just planned
to return. How nice it was to meet you
Ahuda. I hope to see you, and who
knows the future." She said, "I hope so too."

Stanza 91

"Can I see you off tomorrow?" asked
Ahuda "Of course," said Job, happy that
she had asked. He hugged Chara, looking at
Ahuda, then hugged her. *A pleasant
experience* he had thought. "At present,
I must hurry." Job thought, "*A nice contrast
between here and Uz, but perhaps things will
change.* The two women waved goodbye, "Until
we meet again," he yelled to them as he
stepped onto Astra. He looked to see
if Ahuda was watching him—she was.
The morning had been busy: completing
minor repairs on the ships, and loading
the horses; then, coordinating the
boarding of troops and weapons. Ahuda
came to see Job. He was thrilled. "This has
been my lucky day," Job said, as he took
her hand. She said through tears and a sad look,
remembering how the sea had taken
her husband, "I'll pray for you." "You're shaken
by some fear," Job said. "Yes, the deadly sea."
she said. In broken Hebrew to impress
him, "I am happy to meet you." "I guess
this is an omen, he responded. " "Light
will protect us. I have no fear; His might
is ever present with me, and will be.
I am glad that you came to see me." She
hugged him; he embraced her back; she

whispered in his ear, "Please come back to see
me." "I will, much sooner than you think," he
said, and he wanted to kiss her. All of
a sudden she kissed him like a lost love;
she was as lovely as a soft white dove.

CANTO THIRTEEN

Stanza 92

Dark called his commanders to return to
his enthroned being. Let me remind you
Job is a tad lower than the cloned who,
as angelic, as immortals flutter
about—Lights orders of course—utter
control if you will. Men, in fact, are too
much their own predators; evil is a
view point. Any way enough of the
review. We are in a sweet spot, for Job
is about to meet his final fate. Probe
the facts: he is strong, but not enough; he
can fight, but is not invincible; he
will fight the Lotan; surely we will see
him die. This seven headed sea monster
is the last of its kind. Light, the sponsor
of its life, created some, but you see,
he had to make them extinct because of
size and etc. Nothing can shove
him around in or out of the sea. This
is the last Lotan." Airlie asked, "Is
the Lotan your creation like you said?"
"Shut up. Why must you interrupt? O.K.
I did not make the Lotan. What dismay.
What difference does it make?" Dark shouted.
"Where was I? Yes. Job can't kill this touted
gigantic sea dinosaur. It is said

that its height is twenty-one feet tall,
with seven gory heads, below them all
are seven long, powerful necks. The most
horrific creations that are morose—
are on the earth. Where do you think that I get
some of my impersonations? Don't forget,
that our natures are fixed; mine perhaps, not yet."

Stanza 93

"Look at the new love birds; little does she
know that her second love will die at sea.
Ahuda, of course, in the family,
is not as eye-catching as Kallista,
but stunningly beautiful, youthful, ah
don't forget, she is part Hebrew, and she
knows that he liked that facet about her.
Oh well, let's keep eyes on them, as we were,
and the splendid brewing situations
in Kittim, for the prep and foundations
are complete. Damn, I thought that Job would have
been, at least, injured in that crappy, have-
it-your-way, tit-for-tat. Wishful thoughts, save
only that poor Josiah bought it. Phew,
that could have really been tricky—my new
favorite type of killing. Wow, a new knave
approaches; a rebel Greek. Look, he is
admitting blame for the hostilities
to General Job—my god of all things.
The cunning; he has more forces; and sings
like a siren inviting disaster—

wait he is moving them to an island
far from here to fight. "This is Greek heartland,"
he says, "like other city states don't mean
anything—man ever bent to demean.
Job is not worried. Airlie, the faster
that they get on board, the sooner we find
victory. Implicatus is as blind
as a bat with what needs to be done to
rush the loading. Decepticus help to
keep the men thinking about home; women
at home; freedom at home. Get my drift? Men—
led by their male organ—men are men."

Stanza 94

"Tatterius, Decepticus, Airlie,
take any imps you need; follow workers
and listen to what they say, and lurkers
don't count, but they are amusing to tempt;
however, you can find ways to attempt
to hasten along; be creative; be
sure of what you are doing—I mean it.
We're getting to the nitty-gritty. Shit,
the Lotan is prepped: angry to be
alone; upset because he's short of sea
food; and he is out-dated. After he
kills Job, Light will destroy the beast."
Dark and his minions did their work, at least,
they did speed things along. Job's men and work-
men on the dock had other things to work
on when the weekends came, like being free

to fish for food, repair boats or things at
home—or did it feel as though they thought that
they had yearned it. Dark knew the answer.
All aboard, including men. A dancer,
then other dancers with bangles; other
things were shaking as well; all to say thank
you for military aid, and to bank
on them again—if need be; and to say
goodbye. Job felt that currents in the bay
were strangely forceful; so did another
sailor. Job waved; tearful Ahuda
waved as the wind blew her auburn hair—*the
lovely hair*, Job thought. Wind began to kick-
up an hour out. Dark said, "Time to stick
it to them; to kick the crap out of these
ships, with the nice bonus—killing Job. Squeeze
ships closer together. Let's watch—at ease."

Stanza 95

The Great Sea heaved like it was erupting;
the ships now numbered twelve because of new
cargo, items from Kittim; passing through
waters about nine hundred feet from the
shoreline; they were jousted about, then the
sea calmed. The captain, interrupting
Job and another passenger, said, "What
was that?" "Never saw anything that cut
up the sea like that, and then quit," said a
first mate. Everyone was searching when the
sea, suddenly, under the beautiful

sunny sky came something unusual;
a prehistoric fiend; a crucible?
A huge fierce, ugly head lifted out of
the sea; then another head came above;
all with thick long necks; irrefutable
was its anomalous, enormous mass;
nothing the men had feared could surpass
this beast; the skin seemed rough; with odd shapes,
like a parched water bed, and had deep scrapes
or wounds. The body was mostly submerged.
Three of the heads swung about and crashed
into three of the ships. Sailors splashed
into the sea. Pieces of the ship, large,
small, streaked to the sea like a discharge;
immediately men cried for Job; urged
him to do something quickly; he pulled
his sword from his scabbard sprung in curled
position, airborne toward one fiendish
head of the beast with his sword—squeamish-
ness—not in the least. Reaction of a
brave man. He took an eye out of a
head of the closest one of this hydra.

Stanza 96

As Job fought, some parts from the masts and decks
went ninety feet in the air; spewed debris
onto the fleet of ships nearby. The three
cargo ships flew every which way into
the sea. Job struck the head, the jaw, and two
necks, but the blows did nothing. It vexed

him. He slid down the neck striking with his
sword. He landed on the body of this
indomitable creature, but each blow
or stab did not penetrate its hide, so
he dove to what he thought would be tender
tissue, amid leg and body on most
animals; he got there, became engrossed
by what he discovered: huge flat paddle-
type legs; he went up for air. Astraddle
a plank of deck; quickly looked to render
an assessment: the wrecked fleet and the
gross offender; breaths, then back down with the
hope to swim up and stab the soft hide that
was beneath the left back leg socket at
the body—it failed. Anxiety
set in; he prayed to Light: "Save us, oh
sovereign Lord. The behemouth is so
strong and about to kill us all—strike it
down as you have armies before me. Hit
with a holy rage; and definitely
glory and honor will be Yours. Up to
breath, back below; swam straight to
beneath the beast to attack, when Light said,
"All sea hydra that you call beast, are dead,
Except this one. You cannot take its life;
this prehistoric animal, once rife
on this earth. They had been crucial to life."

Stanza 97

"*I* had created it, and all, to show

my omnipotence in the seas. How this
one survived—I kept it alive. This
mammal, no man could kill it." Job said, "What
can I do to save my men, sailors, ships? Rebut
me, yet save them, I'll understand though,
God of my father." No reply as Job
surfaced to view the sea battle; aerobe
he was, needing air more than the hydra;
this time he gasped for air; saliva,
sea water spewed from his mouth. *Where was
Light?* He thought—why not an answer? Because
he now felt that all was a hopeless cause.
Dark said, "Look, I will win because Job is
failing; he is about to succumb; this
challenge is his nemesis; a lost cause
is each human being, incapable
of accomplishing firm exploits, able
to rationalize failure because of
second guessing; then frustration, above
all, leads to questioning Light; giving up
is a natural characteristic
to the majority. Realistic—
Light thinks Job is unique—unlike Adam,
I hope. What had Light been thinking—wait—damn,
Light's plan, this time is destiny; tossup
is out. I am about to find justice,
mercy, grace—good reddens to injustice;
I deserve some slack. Like I said, Light knew
all along that no man could kill this, whew,
indestructible beast. Job is gasping
for air and an answer. Nonetheless—asking

for a second chance at Lucifer—hoping."

Stanza 98

"The last time I had spoken to Light, I
thought that he would, in any case, think on
my case, so that I could find grace. Not on
purely merit." Dark looked at his crew, "All
right, I meant us,"—*not*, he thought; "Good god." All
eyes still on him. "There's no time for this, why
do you question me? Let's discuss Job, that
infernal Job—my god he's a man, drat,
not some angelic god. Never mind; watch
him die. That Lotan will make him botch
the entire encounter. If I slept, I
would now." Light said to Job, "I will kill it
through you. Go to the front right side of it;
under the right front leg is a drainage
vessel; place your sword into the leakage;
it will take most of your arm as well; try
to reach its heart; then twist the sword to the
left, and push. Listen carefully for a
resounding thud, get away as fast as
you are able, for the massive weight has
an uncertain fall as it begins to
drop into the sea." Job swam beneath its
the enormous body to where leg fits
the body; he found the right paddle-like
leg; moved his sword for the precise strike;
found the vessel under a large flap; to
keep holding his breath, he moved quickly;

inserted his sword and arm, and slickly
twisted his sword into the heart. The beast
began to shudder; life in it, decreased
rapidly; a head dropped into the
water next to him to kill him, when the
head of one more missed. Job whispered—"Toda."

Stanza 99

Abruptly, eyes closed on the head, as the
huge body of the beast fell gracefully
toward the murky bottom vacancy.
The Great Sea keeps most of its prey locked
beneath. Job came to the surface; blocked
afternoon sun from his eyes. He saw the
last head tip upward; slip into the water.
Exhausted, grateful, witnessed laughter,
cheers, and praise. He swam to the closest ship—
a wreck. The Lotan had taken a nip
out of his outer thigh with one of its
heads, with a glancing lurch around him; but
the colossal sea beast weighted somewhat
less than nine and a half tons—submerged
to extinction. sailors acknowledged
its existence; Job's men believed in its
deadly menace to man—first hand. Dark said,
"No way. What the hell? I can't get ahead;
this nauseates me. We all knew that the
beast had been impregnable to man, a
common sense thing—god. So, Light tells Job that
there was a flap, under which was a large

fatty drainage vessel; damn, who's in charge?
No one knew—only me and Light. I am,
for once—beside myself. Fuck—it's a sham.
I abhor losing to man. Wait, fail at
this? No. Job didn't win. Light lost—his last
pet dinosaur."Dark sat still. Time passed;
his minions waited for a few minutes.
"The next time Light sends for me; separates
me all in an outer hall—yikes; anyway,
I'll find out what is going on; leeway—
redemption of some kind is still in play."

Stanza 100

"Let's go back to my throne hall, and rethink
our state of affairs. My god life is
perplexing when mistakes live on; this is
a regretful condition—like Adam
and the origin of death to all man-
kind." Dark or Satan or the former fink
angel, Lucifer, led the confused
mass of imps to the dimly lit bemused
fortification. Job saw that only
three ships had survived. Men cold, lonely
on large boards from the wreckage, some not think-
ing clearly, floating, burning up in the
heat; had been in the sea for hours; a
group of boats and two ships were sailing out
of the Kittim Bay to rescue them. Doubt
began to dissipate; a damaged ship began to sink;
joy and relief became the prevailing

moods. Job calmed and assisted ailing
sailors, and men from his army, but he
was held up by many who came to see
him, thanking him; praising him for killing
the sea dragon, and no time to explain
that Light had been the key to the bane
hydra's demise. Within three hours the
rescue ships and boats had arrived; the
men from Kittim had spent hours cleaning
up; preparing to tow the ships that were
repairable back to Kittim—now sure
of their safety—thanks to Job. "It was a
Lotan," called out a captain. All men a-
greed, whether or not they had believed such
a monster existed—there had been much
speculation; at this time—no one said much.

CANTO FOURTEEN

Stanza 101

There was still some trepidation; some thought
that another hydra was somewhere out
in the sea, but Job explained about
Light's final prehistoric animal—
the Lotan; what appeared a rational
killing had not been so, for Light had brought
about the death; I facilitated
the ordeal. Job's anticipated
arrival went throughout the city. His
men and the sailors docked; although his
mind was on Ahuda. Kittim came out
to cheer and to lend a hand with all of
the wounded. Job looked right, left, and above
heads for Ahuda. He found her helping
one of his men. It was overwhelming;
He picked her up in his arms with a shout,
"I love you." She whispered, "You're my hero."
They kissed. He carried her. "Superhero,"
came from the crowd; other adulations
were yelled out with great expectations
of Job living in Kittim. It took three
weeks before ships, crews, and Job's troops were set
to sail to Japho. Job felt sincere debt
to Chara, who had given her blessing
to Ahuda to marry Job, hoping
that they would remain in Kittim. "Agree
with me and I will put together an

expensive dowry," said Chara. "More than
a dowry," Job said, "come to live in Uz?"
"I am not Hebrew." "Light's unchanging laws
accept Gentiles who worship our God.
His ways remain strict, true; although not broad,
He chastises with His love—not a rod."

Stanza 102

Job and Ahuda married—by a priest—
Hebrew; Chara was happy for them, but
was going to miss Ahuda. Somewhat
unhappy, for she'd miss Job too. She thought
about Kallista—only child. Ought
she had gone? Job sailed three hours east
with no problems; so went the voyage. When
they arrived, all residents, Symon
the mayor, other officials, with crowds
everywhere along the docks, beyond. Clouds
could not hide Light's favor toward Job; Light
would soon visit him when he returned to
Uz. Job dismissed his men; said to the crew,
"Job beyond measure." His commanders were
invited to festivities. "The cure
for vexing voyages, and war, tonight
is wine, song, eating," said Symon.
Beautiful Ahuda, seen by women
in Japho, with envy hidden beneath
their joy, while men valued Job's complete
manhood—esteemed by ally and foe
virility, leadership, and daring

in battle, and yet never impairing
another soldier. The men lifted him
as he, with uplifted head, said, "Elohim,
my God, rock, and Savior, from whence flow
strength and power. It's never through my might,
but through Light's does my enemy take flight."
Merriment went on into the night, yet
Job could not keep his thoughts from any threat
of losing her—Ahuda. Gaiety
in his ears as he saw her gracefully
move among the revilers—openly.

Stanza 103

To dismiss his commanders was to be
bittersweet, but there was still much to do
before he had to discharge them. He knew
that they would escort him to Uz, but first,
he had to assure himself that the worst
had passed; only then could he hastily
move ahead, for he longed for peace in
Uz. He believed that Light would begin
a fresh start for him in order to find
rest. He smiled, and went back to the grind
of packing up his own weaponry, some
captured in battle; purchase supplies,
a wagon, team of horses; compromise
nothing when buying few things needed
by Ahuda, or items she had wanted
not a few imported—she would become
his helpmate, lover, and sweet mother of

his children. Amazingly—she's in love
with him. In early afternoon, as Job
finished loading, a man in white robe,
approached, a businessman presented
him with a beautiful Arabian
stallion. His thoughts rushed back to an-
other time to the loud shrill of horn that
signaled charge; courageous men who spat;
blotted out pride, arrogance, and vented
righteousness indignation against the foe
as sword and spear imbibe their blood and woe,
extinguished insolence so that they
could not be consoled; a gloomy day
when not a soldier laments their frenzy;
slaughter is never a choice, for war is deadly,
many guiltless parish—no clemency.

Stanza 104

Job examined his new stallion and
he thought about the uprightness of Light;
Lord of Righteousness: whispered, "Strength and might,
Jehovah Tsidkenu. "What did you say?"
asked the business man. "Just that this day
is a day of gratefulness, yet again."
He agreed that the steed was the most fine-
looking he had ever seen—not a sign
of a blemish. He thanked him. The man
said that he had the horse groomed, as an
extended contribution from the town
and from the entire region for what

Job had done for Japho and Kittim, but
also for opening the trading lanes
in the Great Sea, but not without great pains
and loss. People began shouting around
them, bringing gold and silver coins, trinkets.
Job was grateful but over thinking its
purpose—unlikely. They brought many dried
foods: dates, olives, raisins, pears—fish fried.
Short Habib pushed through the large crowd saying,
"I have brought for you something very sweet."
"You've changed your mind; you are about to treat
us and go along," Job said knowing him
for many years. "No, my friend, broken limb,
but for such a man, I'll be praying."
The man boarded the vessel with his goods,
as others had done. Sailors' livelihoods
had been renewed by the out-poring of
goodness by so many people. "Above
all, come along," exclaimed Ahuda.
"I would like to," said the man, "but, I, ah,
have had evil memories from Uz. Nah."

Stanza 105

Habib had been to Uz when Job had been
ill, due to the twofold test of Light and
Dark, and he desired none of it—grand
though it was to be, according to Job.
Happy was he in Japho, nor would probe
into the affairs of such famed men,
but to say no to Job and Ahuda

was most difficult. Faith in Jehovah
meant that he was to remain in Japho.
The wagons loaded, all set to go,
when three commanders asked to ride ahead.
Job's Arabian stallion was tied to
the back of his wagon; little to do
for three days journey; Ahuda held his
arm close as he drove the team of horses.
When they arrived, Eli met them, said,
"Welcome home brother; house is in order;
repaired by relatives. Disorder
to an appearance of normalcy." They
embraced. Livestock had been their mainstay,
and rebuilding his trading business would
take time. Ahuda was helped down from
the wagon and greeted Eli. "Please, come
into the house. I'll have your things brought in."
Job said that Eli had been the linchpin
around Uz. "He's the eldest of the brood,
and the wisest. His land is an hour
from here." Eli snickered, said, "How're
going to feed your men?" Job said, "I have
some provisions in the wagon, a calf
could be killed, and, of course, we have wine.
Ahuda, everything you see for miles in mine.
Let's cook a feast, invite all, come and dine."

Stanza 106

In the late morning of the next day, faith-
ful commanders gathered by the large barn.

Job had asked them to spend the night. "Farm
or herd is not a bad life," said Haddai,
lead officer. But there's no doubt I'll die
in battle. This last battle has been my eighth."
Friends and family gave Job silver, gold
fine jewels, many animals tenfold
compared to what he had had and they all
spent three days repairing barns on the sprawl
as well as remodeling Job's large house.
The commanders had decided to stay
and work. So quickly had the disarray
been organized that even the men had
been astonished. As badly as it had
been, Uz appeared again as a lighthouse,
a beacon of Light's blessings. Job again
cared for the poor; gave sacrifices when
appropriate; Light had spoken to him
the late evening of the first night back in
Uz, fulfilling his promise to do so.
People came from faraway to visit
the warrior-priest. Years passed, his spirit
remained true to Light; wealth expanded
far beyond expectations; life demanded
more of his time as Ahuda gave birth
to seven sons and three daughters. She would
describe her life as heaven on earth. "Could
I define her beauty? Like a lily;
like a white dove; center of family?"
Warrior-priest, businessman, romantic—
Job was husband and father—authentic.
Tranquility in Uz—optimistic.

www.ingramcontent.com/pod-product-compliance
Lightning Source LLC
LaVergne TN
LVHW041544070426
835507LV00011B/927